FACTORS

Establish the aim, mission, vision, and values of the firm, then manage as an inclusive system—rewarding the whole human being in a way that also rewards the firm.

Create a permeable organization structure and interactive management processes in an open, trusting environment—for learning on the job and as multiplier of formal training and education.

Understand and communicate the interdependence of all components.

Conduct an audit of formal and informal measurements and controls. Eliminate noise—defined as information that does not contribute to the central mission of the firm, which is to profitably design, build, and sell a product or service.

Remove violators from the system, swiftly and summarily. Eliminate conditions that might cause recurrence.

T
R
U
S
T

The Trust Factor

Liberating Profits and Restoring Corporate Vitality

John O. Whitney

McGraw-Hill, Inc.

New York   San Francisco   Washington, D.C.   Auckland   Bogotá
Caracas   Lisbon   London   Madrid   Mexico City   Milan
Montreal   New Delhi   San Juan   Singapore
Sydney   Tokyo   Toronto

Library of Congress Cataloging-in-Publication Data

Whitney, John O.
    The trust factor : liberating profits and restoring corporate
vitality / John O. Whitney.
        p.   cm.
    Includes index.
    ISBN 0-07-070017-6 (alk. paper)
    1. Management. 2. Trust (Psychology). I. Title.
HD38.W4266 1993
658—dc20   93-28028
                                             CIP

1 2 3 4 5 6 7 8 9 0 DOC/DOC 9 9 8 7 6 5 4 3

ISBN 0-07-070017-6

*The sponsoring editor for this book was Betsy N. Brown, the editing supervisor
was Stephen M. Smith, and the production supervisor was Pamela A. Pelton.
It was set in Palatino by McGraw-Hill's Professional Book Group composition
unit.*

Printed and bound by R. R. Donnelley & Sons Company.

This book is printed on recycled, acid-free paper
containing a minimum of 50% recycled de-inked fiber.

This book is dedicated to three wise men: Olney A. Whitney, who taught me respect for learning; Professor Franklin J. Eikenberry, who taught me respect for the English language; and Dr. W. Edwards Deming, whose theory of profound knowledge changed the course of my professional life

Contents

Foreword

by W. Edwards Deming

We have reached the limits of the capability of our current philosophy and resulting methods of management. American Industry, our services, our government, and our education are today in an invisible prison. The walls of the prison are the basic assumptions that are made today about economics and human behavior. They are outmoded in the global economy of this day. We can emerge from this prison only through knowledge that is not a part of the present system. This knowledge may be described as Profound Knowledge. The result of adoption and application of Profound Knowledge is transformation of the individual. The individual, transformed, has a basis for his own life and decisions, and a basis for judgment and suggestions for other people's actions.

A key element of Profound Knowledge is the concept and application of the theory of a system. A system is a network of interdependent components that work together to accomplish the aim of the system. A business is a complex system. All of the components—research and development, sales, manufacturing, etc.—are interdependent and must work together to produce products and services that accomplish the aim of the system.

Optimization for accomplishment of the aim of a system requires cooperation between the components of the system. Left to themselves in the Western world, components become selfish, competitive, independent profit centers. An organization must accordingly be managed.

The cost of mistrust is one of the losses to business and to society in the Western world that can not be measured. There is the unmeasurable psychological cost of anxiety, and of layers of inspection to test conformance to agreement.

The most important losses can not be measured, yet these are the losses that for survival we must manage (a principle stated years ago by Lloyd S. Nelson).

Trust is mandatory for optimization of a system. Without trust, there can not be cooperation between people, teams, departments, divisions. Without trust, each component will protect its own immediate interests to its own long-term detriment, and to the detriment of the entire system. Transformation is required. This means adoption and integration of new principles.

Transformation begins with the individual. The job of a leader is to create an environment of trust so that everyone may confidently examine himself.

Professor Whitney brings home, in concrete fashion, the tremendous costs of the prevailing system of management. He helps us examine our current systems to see how lack of trust adversely affects today every aspect of our business. He helps us to look through the lens of Profound Knowledge so that we may begin to manage our organizations in a spirit of cooperation, win-win.

Mistrust is the basic reason for procedures drawn up in great detail, often 30 or 40 or more pages, for any agreement or transaction in business, whether it be simple or complex.

In contrast, two Japanese companies would draw up an agreement in one or two pages, with phrases such as "details to be worked out later, if need arise." It is understood without comment that the basis for working out the details later would be win-win, neither party to be a loser. We could learn a lot from Japan.

W. E. D.
May 1993

Preface

For the past 20 years, I have been involved with business turnarounds. Fourteen of those years, I was a CEO, COO, or chairman. The past seven years, I have been a professor of management, teaching the corporate turnarounds course at Columbia Business School. And, for the past three years, I have also served as director of the W. Edwards Deming Center for Quality Management at Columbia. One might naturally ask, "What do turnarounds, trust, and Dr. Deming have in common?" In a word, everything. A sustainable business turnaround is more than firing people, divesting companies, or practicing financial engineering. If the recovering company cannot soon stand toe-to-toe with world-class competitors, its agony will have been all for naught. Many of its competitors will have been influenced by the theories of Dr. Deming, who, as most people know, was an architect of history's most astonishing economic turnaround—Japan after World War II and until the late 1980s. Although Japan is having serious economic difficulties in the 1990s, few analysts believe these difficulties are the result of the operating management methods introduced by Dr. Deming.

As for trust, Kenneth Arrow, the Nobel laureate, has said that it is the lubricant of society.[1] In business turnarounds as well as leading-edge companies, trust is not only the lubricant that helps get things done, it is also the glue that holds the organization to-gether.

Trust might seem to be an unusual organizational attribute. But it is well known to those who have led successful operational turnarounds. After the agonizing period of downsizing and di-vestiture is complete, the turnaround leader quickly assembles a group of people whom he or she trusts. The leader works with them to establish appropriate goals, then turns them loose with no red tape and a minimum of control. Furthermore, the leader sees to it that an aura of trust radiates from the core group through the entire organization. The troubled company cannot afford mistrust. It cannot afford to sap people's energies by re-quiring them to constantly outwit a tar pit bureaucracy. It cannot afford a towering organization structure and stove-pipe func-tions with the attendant excesses of inspection, supervision, checks, balances, reports, and controls. If it does not unburden it-self of this baggage, it will provide full employment for the next decade's crop of turnaround specialists.

This warning is not idle speculation. It is the result of my study of hundreds of businesses, large and small, troubled and presently untroubled. My conclusions are based on the following premises:

If the function of business is to profitably design, build, and sell a product or service, then about half of its activities are unneces-sary. Put another way: Costs are about double the optimum. Moreover, wasted activities and unnecessary complexity sap the creative energy and the motivation of the people doing the work, a cost that is not measurable. If these premises seem extreme, con-sider your answers to the following—either for your organization or for business in general.

1. Are administrative costs increasing faster than revenue growth?
2. Are selling and marketing costs increasing faster than revenue growth?
3. Is time-to-market competitive?
4. Are new products or services meeting or exceeding customer expectations?

5. Is the entire organization focused on the customer, or is it generally focused inward on relationships among its own members?

Current business performance suggests that answers to these questions would be unsatisfactory. Many business giants are in decline. Economies of scale and scope seem now to be diseconomies. Small organizations appear with great promise, soar for a while, then too many gradually decline or, worse, crash and burn. The premise holds true even for businesses that have downsized. If they have not removed unnecessary activities and unleashed the creative potential of the people who remain, these businesses find that they must downsize again and again—sometimes into oblivion.

Nothing is really new here. Disasters like these are reported daily in the business press. But if the problems are well known, the real causes apparently are not. Quite often the blame is laid on external forces: technological, regulatory, or environmental changes, and competitive activities. These are reasons, not excuses. External factors apply to everyone. Companies with low cost structures that retain the ability to move quickly with leading-edge products and services welcome change in the external environment. But for companies whose costs are too high and whose competitive edge is dulled and whose response is slow, change is frightening; existence for them is difficult, even in a benign environment.

My earlier assertion that 50 percent of our activities are wasted might be conservative. George Stalk and Tom Hout, the pundits of time-based management, report: "Most products and many services are actually receiving value for only .05 to 5 percent of the time that they are in the value delivery system of their companies."[2] Mike Hammer, the guru of reengineering, reported his now-legendary example of the 80 percent reduction in the accounts payable work force at Ford Motor Company.[3] Tim Fuller, who studies complexity in business organizations, reported work-sampling observations of an assembly operation in which 43 percent of the activities were real work. The rest was unnecessary complexity.[4] Tom Peters in *Liberation Management* reports on the famed Asea Brown Boveri firm, which believes the headquarters staff of most activities can be reduced by 90 percent in the first year. ABB runs a company which in 1991 had $28.9 billion in revenues, with only three layers of management. Peters reports similar results in the Titeflex Company.[5] My experience as a work-out consultant at the appliance division of General Electric confirms these observations. GE is probably the best-led large company in the world, but its administrative activities, effective as they are, still are too burdensome.

Many companies address administrative waste by applying techniques like process mapping, flow charting, town meetings, and thinking "outside the box." Others bulldoze waste and complexity out of the enterprise. All these streamlining activities are necessary and commendable. Some will endure because they are directly or indirectly addressing causes as well as symptoms. But others will have their brief moments in the sun, then fade away, because they have treated symptoms only. Processes that have been reengineered will be replaced by processes that look like the ones that have existed before the reengineering consultant arrived. Time and complexity will creep back into those processes and those systems. Managers and employees will burn out, become disillusioned, or leave the enterprise.

Mistrust is the cause that must be addressed if these process improvements are to endure. We do not usually trust the competence and motives of others. Sometimes we do not trust their integrity. We do not trust information—especially the financial and accounting reports. To protect ourselves, we build fortresses: extra measurements and controls, reviews, meetings, memos, and documentation. We break jobs into smaller pieces, then we add layers of supervision. We add inspectors. We tinker with incentive and reward systems. We centralize, then decentralize. We alternate between delegation, abdication, and micromanagement. When all else fails, we transfer or terminate management and employees. Defensive measures like these will not support enduring improvement.

Perhaps analytical business people are reluctant to address trust and mistrust because these concepts seem too soft. "Give us something hard and substantive, not something fuzzy like trust." Their reluctance is vindicated also by the realization that much mistrust is well placed. People are often incompetent. Their motives often clash with ours and with the firm's. Sometimes they lie, cheat, and steal. The financial information they provide is often late, wrong, or irrelevant.

Reluctance to address trust might be eased, however, if we were to acknowledge that trust in business is not like Portia's mercy, which "droppeth as the gentle rain from heaven." On the contrary, in order to trust we must first mistrust. Enduring trust must be earned—up, down, and across the organization. How it is earned, preserved, and used to reduce waste and eliminate unnecessary complexity, how it is used to improve the vitality of the firm and its products and services, is the subject of our enquiry.

John O. Whitney

Acknowledgments

My first meeting with Dr. W. Edwards Deming was a pivotal event in my professional life. That meeting in 1987 prompted a warm friendship and, for me, a continuing intellectual challenge. Many of the propositions I advance in this book will be familiar to those who have studied with Dr. Deming. They will understand my profound debt to him—in almost every chapter. But no one speaks for W. Edwards Deming. His voluminous writing and public statements speak for themselves. His recent book, *The New Economics for Industry, Government, Education*,[1] will set a standard for years to come. If the ideas here are credible, many of the plaudits go to him; if not, the blame to me.

The other two men to whom the book is dedicated also had a powerful influence on my life. My father was a school principal in southeastern Oklahoma during the depths of the Great Depression. School pay was so low that he moved to the oil fields, then on to oil company headquarters; but his love of learning never left him, and he held it high for me to see. Franklin Eikenberry was professor of English at Tulsa University. His specialty was the Shakespeare history plays, in which he was so steeped that his lectures seemed to be in perfect Elizabethan blank verse. Blank verse or not, Shakespeare's lessons in leadership sprang to life under Professor Eikenberry's tutelage. The good professor made another contribution. He once suggested that if I wished to truly appreciate the English language I should write a sonnet a day. I produced a semester of the world's worst sonnets but did learn to appreciate the English language.

Professor John O'Shaughnessy, the most literate man I know, challenged some of my incendiary assertions, causing me to offer a more balanced discussion which, in my view, made my case stronger and more believable. He also diverted the muzzle from my foot in several instances where I had an imperfect understanding of the antecedents of the theories I had cited. Moreover, he provided a comprehensive written critique, which profoundly influenced the finished manuscript.

Michael F. Young, Esq., of Willkie Farr & Gallagher, with whom I have worked and who I have come to respect as a brilliant lawyer and as a razor-sharp intellect, provided tough criticism and enthusiastic support. I shall always cherish two of his marginal notations: "Whitney, you don't know what you're talking about" and "I just hate this chapter." The offending section and chapter were tossed out. The book is better for the expurgations.

Robert Lear, former CEO, author, and Executive-in-Residence at Columbia, provided insight and support as he always does. His written critique was most helpful. Charles Clough, CEO of Nashua Corporation, reviewed and commented on the manuscript. Moreover, he and three of his senior managers with whom I have also worked—Joe Kershaw, Bob Geiger, and Frank Faticanti—have tested many of the ideas presented here.

Mark Graham, research assistant for the Deming Lecture Series that I offer at Columbia, provided detailed suggestions, most of which were incorporated in the final draft. Kenneth Craddock, senior teaching assistant for the Deming Lectures, commented on the manuscript and continually fed me with new material. Professor Murray Low commented on an early draft and made valuable suggestions about the book's organization. Professor Danny Miller at the Ecole des Hautes Etudes Commerciales in Montreal provided enthusiastic support as well as valuable advice that gave balance to some of my more controversial arguments. Professors Casey Ichniowski and Joel Brockner at Columbia Business School and Professor Donald Morrison at UCLA read portions of the manuscript and supported the central ideas in the book.

I have the honor of serving as pro bono advisor of some departments of the U.S. Navy and have received feedback on these ideas from them. Special thanks go to Admiral Jim Miller and Admiral Don Weatherston and their associates. Former Undersecretary of the Navy, The Honorable Daniel J. Howard, is probably the most knowledgable man in America on the subject of introducing quality management practices in large organizations. He offered valuable advice and support.

Three of the people who are closest to Dr. Deming, Drs. Barbara Lawton, Nida Backaitis, and Joyce Orsini, have contributed substantially to my understanding of Dr. Deming's theories. I owe much to Professor Peter Kolesar, who teaches a Columbia Business School course on the management of quality and who first introduced me to Dr. Deming. Professor Robert Howell, a colleague years ago at the Harvard Business School, now a professor at New York University and a preeminent figure in the new wave of management accounting, influenced many of my recommendations in the chapter on measurement.

Professor Jim Kuhn of Columbia might have started it all during a discussion of business ethics, when he remarked, "Think of what mistrust costs us." Professor Nathaniel Leff has shared with me his own work on trust but has also faithfully sent other material that contributed to the book's central arguments. Geoffrey Heal, professor and vice dean at Columbia Business School, put me on the trail of readings in transaction theory. Professors John Donaldson and Bill Lehr have also shared their insights. Professor E. Kirby Warren, with whom I have worked on assignments at General Electric, brought fine insight into how one preserves the good in organizations while excising the bad. He also made extensive and helpful comments on early chapters. Professor Kathy Harrigan's work on strategy for mature industries continues to provide important insights.

My humble thanks go to business leaders who have been subjected to these theories during their development over the past three years. Well over a thousand men and women at Columbia's executive seminars have shot arrows and thrown bouquets. Both were appreciated, but the arrows were more useful—they caused me to sharpen or change my thinking. Similarly, the hundreds of people at GE Appliances as well as

GE's corporate managers have contributed enormously to my insights, as have executives at TRW Space and Defense sector, Grand Metropolitan plc, The Nashua Corporation, GROWMARK Inc., W. R. Grace, Avon Products, Bristol-Myers Squibb, and dozens of others with whom I have had short encounters. My experience as a manager of business turnarounds has also honed my perceptions. I thank the heroes in these encounters and nod to the villians. I learned from both.

Betsy Brown, senior editor at McGraw-Hill, provided excellent, timely editorial guidance. Marcia Whitney, as always, kept me focused, and her incisive comments brought me from the ether back to reality. Marcia and I both express our enormous debt to Joy Glazener, who not only turned my foolscap into type but who offered insights as well as encouragement. Her contributions were enormous.

Special thanks go to David John Sainsbury, Chairman and CEO of J. Sainsbury plc, whose business leadership has been inspirational and whose faith in the Columbia Business School prompted his initial contribution to the Deming Center.

In considering the massive help and encouragement from my colleagues over the past three years, I probably should be reluctant to put my name on the book, but many of my constructs might be controversial enough that my colleagues will be happy to remain as advisors merely. Indebted as I am, I nevertheless shield them from unwarranted criticism by assuming full responsibility for the ideas and words that follow.

Introduction

1

Trust and the Bottom Line

Sounds crass, doesn't it? Equating trust—a moral, ethical concept—so directly with profit and loss. Virtue is supposed to be its own reward—agreed. But virtue and profits are not mutually exclusive. Consider the following questions:

If everyone in your organization knew what to do; when, how, where to do it—and, most important, why he was doing it—what would the organization chart look like?

If everyone desired to do his job correctly, on time, *and* could be trusted to act with integrity in support of the firm's aims and goals, what would your organizational process and control systems be like?

The answers are straightforward. The organization structure would be flatter, supervisors fewer; numbing sign-off, control, and measurement systems that require armies of line and support personnel would disappear. Profits would soar.

In seminars for senior executives, I often begin with the contentious statement: "Half the work going on in your company today is wasted, and half of your workforce may be unnecessary, even if you have recently reorganized or downsized." By noon, their low growls have turned to muted murmurs and by 5 p.m. those murmurs have turned to genuine enquiry. During the day, the executives will have pondered the following.

Management
Anachronisms

"How long does it take to make a simple change in a manufacturing process?" One company learned that if the approvals, sign-offs, cross-checks, and other controls were followed precisely, a simple screw change would take 7 months. Happily, the company's managers and employees had the good sense to break the rules and shorten the process considerably.

"How much executive time is spent in budgeting, rebudgeting, forecasting, reforecasting, justifying, defending—then assigning blame?" What starts this chain reaction? Substandard performance or unrealistic projections driven by fear of the consequences of sticking with an honest appraisal? For example, if the initial budget projections seem too low, are they papered over with optimistic sales forecasts and prayerful cost reduction targets? How much better if the weeks and months wasted in torturing the numbers into an acceptable outcome were spent on fixing the problems. Admittedly, budgets are usually supported by an action plan which demonstrates how the objectives will be achieved. But in the hurly-burly, these problems are pushed aside, typically until midway through the third quarter. It is usually at this point that managers wish they could recapture the time they had spent on budgeting so they could have started corrective actions earlier. Instead, they fall back on typical fourth-quarter crisis management. Advertising, maintenance, training, travel are curtailed; Christmas layoffs and other morale builders are announced in part because trust has taken a holiday.

"How many management layers in your accounts payable department?" One embarrassed controller answered "four." When pressed, he agreed that the function of his middle managers was not to train, integrate, and coordinate but to control. These managers were inspectors—police—giving clear signals that lowly clerks could not be trusted to make decisions. This controller then studied a self-supervised payables group that had been provided the training and tools that gave them the knowledge that enabled them to decide and then act. The group that he studied had only one management layer. It was achieving 40 percent greater output with one-half the head count of the firm's traditional department.

"How much time is wasted because insecure managers discourage or forbid subordinates from talking directly to their counterparts in other functions?" They insist on knowing, in detail, everything that happens—insisting that all communication travel up and down the chain of command. I have seen sales and marketing executives in a war so fierce that subordinates were told to communicate only by memos, which first had to be cleared by supervisors. In another instance, a senior research scientist recounted that he almost lost his job because he communicated directly with a production engineer, not to change a process but merely to ask for information! These are extreme examples, but the knowing looks exchanged by managers when I recite these examples indicate that they are not entirely farfetched.

"How much time is wasted managing multiple sourcing relationships when the situation calls for one or two value-added suppliers?" Think of the time lost managing the bidding process! Think of the extra time-to-market and potential quality loss when one fails to use the special knowledge of a trusted supplier for design or tooling help or in solving a tough manufacturing problem.

The consultants that were helping a large retail firm to reduce its costs stumbled onto a remote division's boot-legged IBM System 38 which ran its own reports because the division did not trust the pricing and cost information generated at headquarters. Think of the direct costs of this redundant activity. More important, think of the indirect costs.

Here are others: Does your company require approval of executive expense accounts? How many signatures? One? Two? More? When did you last turn one down?

Expense account approvals might be necessary in some environments, but as a turnaround manager I have found that when people understand the financial situation and the basic guidelines, they will control their expenses much more effectively than rigid rules and a zealous controller.

How many signatures required on time cards? Travel requests? Purchase orders?

Are you sometimes required to sign off on something because of your management position? Do you really know what you are signing? Has the work ever been delayed because you were busy or out of town? Did you try to calculate the cost of the delay—in out-of-pocket costs or in loss of market position?

People Are No Damn Good—a Flawed Premise

Earlier, I stated that mistrust is sometimes well-placed and that trust must be earned. These statements may seem to conflict with my view here that people basically wish to cooperate, to contribute, to feel that they belong to a socioeconomic system (macro and micro) that serves mankind. The earlier cautionary admonitions are justified because of the exceptions: There are those who would cheerfully cut our throats. In addition, there are those who would like to cooperate but do not know how. Furthermore, there are many with excellent intentions but whose goals may be incongruent with ours or with those of the enterprise. As for the first group, those whose intentions are malevolent, the effort to bring them around usually is neither effective nor efficient. A good offense or a strong defense may be more salutary. The danger, however, is that we generalize from these exceptions into a deep distrust of those who wish to cooperate but don't know how and those whose intentions are good but whose goals may be incongruent.

The flawed premise that lumps all three of these together triggers costly and enduring protective mechanisms and masks the opportunity to remove root causes. It blinds us to the realization that most people have an intrinsic pride in work and accomplishment which, when tapped, can reduce the need for cumbersome, often demeaning, control systems.

Three caricatures of managers' views of human nature illustrate the difficulties that we face in arriving at an acceptable theory about humans in the workplace. Harry Levinson's book, *The Great Jackass Fallacy*, satirizes the carrot-and-stick school of management where a carrot is tied to the end of a long stick which is then secured to a donkey's back so the carrot dangles tantalizingly in front of its nose.[1] Combining this primitive view with a more moderate one, some wag has developed "Theory Y-Prime" which states, "Beat the workers with a big carrot." Finally, the old maxim from the U.S. Army World War II leadership school, "You can *ex*pect what you *in*spect." In short, people are greedy, apathetic, unambitious, childish, selfish, dumb, and lazy. They grudgingly do what they are told—no more, sometimes less. When they finish their work they wouldn't think of helping someone else. They don't care about the company. All they want is more coffee breaks, more sick days, longer vacations, shorter workweeks, and more money. Overblown? Certainly! No twentieth-century managers in their right minds really believe that the foregoing accurately characterizes human nature—but their management methods, practices, and policies sometimes belie it. The command and control concept, perhaps necessary to goad a sullen army into the fray, has influenced our organizational design and our management to the extent that trust has been trampled. Another wag has said, "If you're looking for trust, you can find it in the dictionary—somewhere between trauma and truth." Another frustrated manager put it, "Yes, I trust everyone—to look out for his or her own self-interest."

The late and otherwise revered Dr. Kaoru Ishikawa was excoriated for his statement, "The basic teachings of Christianity appear to say that man is, by nature, evil."[2] Even his translator disassociated himself from the statement. Dr. Ishikawa supported his thesis with the example that 15 percent of U.S. factory workers—compared to 1 percent of Japanese workers—are inspectors. (Subsequent studies have shown an even higher cost for inspection.) Ishikawa went on to say that this suggested that people cannot be trusted. He characterized our attitudes with the statement "Therefore, [in the West] the division of inspection and quality control must be independent and given even greater power. Without this power to observe and inspect there can be no quality assurance. This attitude is clearly a manifestation of a theory that man is, by nature, evil." Farfetched? Possibly. Ishikawa buttressed his argument with other examples, but whether one agrees or disagrees with the diagnosis, it is dangerous to ignore the symptoms.

Perhaps the words are wrong, but the tune is familiar. We do not trust people to submit honest expense accounts. We have time clocks to ensure that employees report hours correctly. We treat most insurance claims as if they are fabricated. We are reluctant to give praise for fear that the recipient will demand a favor. Our retailing establishments have elaborate bureaucracies to control inventory shrinkage. One food store manager directed that all store doors be locked while the night restockers were working. Doors were reopened in the morning by a security officer. It may have been cheaper, albeit unacceptable, to let each worker filch a case of salmon rather than to cause the morale problems and attendant productivity loss the locked door environment would engender.

As I said earlier, the foregoing is not to suggest that we suddenly act as if everyone's heart was pure, intentions honorable, and honesty unimpeachable. Some employees and customers do steal from stores. Some managers do cheat on expense accounts. Some suppliers have gouged their customers through substandard quality, fraudulent billing, and delivery promises that were broken before they were made. Employees often "put in their time" looking for every opportunity to shirk. In extreme cases they are malicious, sabotaging both the output and the process. Moreover, these attributes differ geographically. In our inner cities, some businesses are run as virtual police states by desperate owners and managers trying to cope. Society has dealt the cards, and businesses play the hands as best they can. Others use the harsh environment as an excuse to cheat customers not wily or strong enough to protect themselves.

Ben Franklin did not exude faith in human nature when he said, "If we got what we deserved, we would all hang." Perhaps businesses have been getting the trust they deserve. For instance, managers destroy trust when they establish unachievable quotas to goad people to increase output. Sure, the goods may get to the shipping door but quality goes out the window—and the workers know it. What about other games that are played—which employees and managers know are being played—in order to meet the numbers? Borrowing sales from next quarter. Slowing down this quarter because we have made quota. Shipping an order we know will be returned. Sharpening up the silver pencil, capitalizing instead of expensing, failing to take timely write-downs and reserves, switching from LIFO to FIFO and vice versa, not to reduce taxes but to influence reported earnings. Not only do managers distrust employees, but employees distrust managers, and both distrust the information that they are getting.

What's to be done? Tighten the screws? Pass more laws? Produce more reports? Make unions more militant? Hire more police and inspectors? These purported solutions run counter to the theory of holes: If you want to get out, stop digging!

Pride in Work

The time has come for management practices to reflect more productive assumptions about human nature. In addition to the questions about competence and trust which were posed at the beginning, consider this rather strange query:

> If pride in work or accomplishment, rather than profit maximization, were the driving motivation of the firm, would your profits be more or less?

People spend most of their working lives performing or thinking about their work. Given half a chance, they want to be productive. They want to produce high-quality products or provide excellent service. They want to be proud of their companies, bosses, and associates—and most of all, themselves. Of course, pride alone will not produce profits. There must also be functional competence, reasonable systems of administration, and a sense of mission that pulls people in the same direction. But many executives who have pondered the question respond, "If we produced products and services of which we were all justifiably proud, our sales would be higher. And if we could eliminate bureaucratic systems and procedures which not only waste time but also rob people of their dignity and discourage their creativity, costs would be lower." A pretty good equation for higher profits!

The power of pride and accomplishment was brought home to me when I led a large supermarket chain whose employees had organized a league of 92 softball teams—a daunting task of planning, logistics, and scheduling. I marvelled at the enthusiasm that they brought to the task and was astounded at their efficiency. They spent a few hours a week of their own time to manage the project. The company provided the equipment and got out of the way. I then pondered long and hard over the question, "What if we got out of their way in our distribution centers and our stores?" Answering that question helped me to eliminate a lot of nonsense which had passed for control and reporting procedures.

Pride in work is not reserved for hobbies and intramural activities. Nor is it reserved for those with the prestigious jobs and the best education. I have seen managers and workers in so-called urban ghetto stores in New York's Bronx outperform their counterparts in more genteel areas. And I have seen them do it with enthusiasm and pride. They were successful in part because they trusted their manager and he trusted them. I have seen the manager storm into headquarters protesting an asinine central directive that would unfairly affect his people, and I have seen his employees rally around him when times got tough. The store outperformed all its counterparts in productivity and profitability—in large measure because the people respected each other: They reinforced that respect with their management methods and work ethic—and, most of all, they had pride in their work. They eagerly awaited visits from headquarters because they and their stores were "standing tall." These employees believed that they were integral to the business, not just human resource inputs.

Stories like these exist throughout corporate America in enterprises large and small. They are the exception, not the rule. They usually occur because a group of heroes have transcended outmoded management methods and theories of human behavior. Stories like these should no longer be grist for books on "excellence." They should be commonplace. When they become commonplace, we will have marched into a world of economic plenty and, more importantly, a world where the creative potential of workers and managers will be fully realized. On a more commercial note we will be in a world where pride in work will be an analog for profits and growth.

Utopian? Certainly. The millennium will not be realized in my lifetime, nor my son's and daughter's, but we can begin.

External Costs of Mistrust

The examples above demonstrate excessive internal costs. To dramatize the importance of trust in all business relationships, let us look briefly at well-known examples of excessive external costs among firms or between the firm and its customer.

When customers lose faith, selling costs soar, and sales curves plunge. Consider the announcement by Salomon Brothers that its most senior officers had resigned because they had not disclosed violations of bond-trading rules in a timely manner. Following that announcement, management was focused on damage control. Instantly, this great money machine had been thrown into reverse. Long-term projects, new products and services, sales efforts to new important customers halted. But operating costs went on and legal costs skyrocketed.

During Drexel Lambert's last month before filing for Chapter 11, money hemorrhaged while the company's officers fought to restore credibility. In the spring of 1984, people lost confidence in Continental Bank of Chicago. Money poured out. Very little new money came in. The bank had to be rescued. The savings and loan crisis wiped out the FSLIC. The epidemic of bank failures has almost wiped out the FDIC. Now we must put our trust in Congress. Small comfort there.

Scandals in fiduciary institutions dramatize the economics of trust. Establishing, maintaining, and restoring trust for any firm— bank or not—is a crucial and costly task. An important consulting firm had its jousts with trust in the executive office, resulting in the resignation of the founder and other senior executives. Precious few new consulting projects were acquired, and many of America's best and brightest left the firm voluntarily and involuntarily. Billable hours of the survivors were difficult to come by, as some of the finest minds in the world focused their efforts not on growing but on surviving. The firm is now successful and growing again, but it lost two long years and hundreds of quarts of blood.

U.S. automobile companies have in the past few years made great strides toward gaining consumer confidence but are still paying dearly as the companies try to restore the trust they lost in the 1970s and 1980s. Automobile size and fuel economy contributed to their problems, but lack of reliability was also important. Too many things went wrong with cars. Foreign competitors made a car that could be trusted to get there and back. Today, most U.S. cars are quite reliable, and styling is improving. But the overall loss in momentum has cost billions.

Time was that we could pick up the telephone with complete confidence that we would complete our call. We can still complete calls with an incredibly high degree of confidence, but the two or three serious and well-publicized system failures in 1990 and 1991 shook that confidence, opened the doors to competitive attacks, and made AT&T's sales job much more difficult.

Publicity about Medicaid and Medicare fraud and other billing excesses has labeled physicians as money-grubbers, not the caring souls characterized by the Hippocratic oath. Thousands of thoughtful, caring physicians have paid a dear price for those who have broken the trust.

Nor has higher education escaped. Dr. John A. White, former assistant director of the National Science Foundation, and now dean of the College of Engineering at Georgia Tech, told a conference of academics and senior corporate executives that the education crisis may loom as large as the savings and loan crisis.[3] We academics have lost the confidence of many of our important constituencies, one of which is the U.S. corporation. Many of our corporate supporters believe that our teaching has deteriorated, our curricula are outdated, and our research largely irrelevant. As usual, there is merit on both sides. To the consternation of some of my academic friends, I believe that the weight of the argument is now on business's side. But what I or my colleagues think makes very little difference in terms of the trust relationship. If we are wrong, we must change. If we are right, we must be more effective in communicating our position. If, however, we can jump neither of these hurdles, we richly deserve the consequences, even if our students do not. The point is that when trust is diminished, supporters are less eager to hire our graduates, build our buildings, underwrite our research, or support our curriculum and teaching.

There are instances where loss of trust is clearly undeserved. The bogus alar scare nearly ruined the apple industry. Back in the 1960s, the cranberry scare had disastrous effects on the cranberry industry. These days there's an ironic twist to these events. Some consumers have become weary of the annual food scare and are impugning the motives of professional environmentalists, some of whom seem to have more interest in a political than a consumerist agenda. They too might learn that trust is ephemeral: hard to get but easy to lose.

Adversarial Activity or Advocacy?

Whether mistrust is external to the firm or inside the firm, it usually generates adversarial activities. These activities might sharpen the mind, but they rarely put bread on the table. Inside the firm, they spawn a hierarchy of managers whose job it is to inspect and control. In the external world, they spawn a crippling maze of laws and regulations. Whether these artifacts of mistrust spring from assumptions about human nature that were mentioned earlier, whether they are imposed by flawed assumptions about truth-seeking, or whether they persist because of our management methods, policies, and procedures is unclear to me; but the adversarial activity is such an important cause of economic waste that it deserves a closer look.

Earlier, I aimed a barb at Congress. Is politician-baiting a cruel sport or deserved retribution? Only rarely do we trust our political leaders, even when they are truly dedicated public servants. The reasons are complex, but one of the leading causes is the trampling of trust by adversarial proceedings, in which most politicians are well schooled. Consider the traditional political debate. One side makes the strongest possible case for its point, offering only evidence that supports that position. The other side uses the same strategy—offering only the evidence that supports its case.[4] Adversary theory holds that the truth should emerge from the argument. The inescapable conclusion, however, is that both debaters are liars. How could it be otherwise? Neither has told *the* truth. *A* truth may slip out from time to time, but *the* truths remain hidden in the polemic. One or the other may win according to the rules of debate, but neither wins the trust of the constituents.

Here a distinction should be drawn between adversarial activity and advocacy. Effective advocates can help to ensure that issues on both sides of an argument are identified and carefully considered. Effective advocacy can also ensure against compromise that so muddles an issue or course of action that neither side nor the cause is well served. The difference between adversarial activity and advocacy that I propose turns on whether the objective is aggrandizement of self-interest or enhancement of the enterprise.

Politicians are not alone in contributing to lost confidence. Business, to its detriment, has sometimes failed to make the distinction. It has, perhaps unwittingly, fostered self-interested adversarial tenets rather than advocacy through the presumption that its activities are zero-sum—for every winner, there must be a loser. Thus the executive who wins the resource allocation argument is lionized. The loser is punished—not overtly, but in loss of stature and influence. But if the decision is beneficial to the enterprise, the notion of winners and losers is spurious. Both executives should be winners. Yet some unwitting perversity seems to drive us to the zero-sum paradigm that prescribes competition rather than cooperation. Perhaps the most perverse effect of the paradigm is the practice of forced ranking of employees or the annual merit review mandate that no more than 20 percent of the people can be rated as outstanding. Not only does this foster adversarial behavior, but it is foolish. I have seen instances in which none of the employees was truly competent. I have seen other instances in which all were competent; moreover, they functioned as an effective team. Rating 20 percent of them as outstanding and another 20 percent as unsatisfactory would have destroyed their effectiveness. It would have created waste and complexity and would have diverted the energy of the firm to unproductive work. Senior managers should therefore be alert to the occasions when subordinates are engaged in political or seemingly ideological struggles with each other; then, rather than ascribe that behavior to "human nature," managers should seek out and remove the causes. An enterprise that is at war with itself will not have the strength or the focus to survive and thrive in today's competitive environment.

2
Trust and Mistrust

The trust most needed by organizations is trust that is earned, then cherished. In some respects, it is akin to trust among Marines or any battle unit that has trained together and has met and conquered adversity on the training field or battleground. It is the trust that if one of their number is wounded, none will rest until he is rescued; if someone is killed, his body will be recovered so it can be buried with dignity. Carried to excess, however, this construction of trust can be chauvinistic, exclusionary, and dangerously arrogant. It is most suited for crises. It runs the risk of blinding one to opportunities where the goals are more complex than immediate survival. Nonetheless, its salutary characteristics—a sense of brotherhood, sharing, and justice—would go far to reduce the waste and to liberate the creative energies of those who now are trapped in some of our bureaucratic tar pits.

Trust also exists among professionals, conditioned not by any particular sense of brotherhood—but by respect for competence and reliability. These are necessary but insufficient conditions for trust within organizations where interdependence suggests a need for justice and fairness in addition to competence and reliability. Integrity, of course, is a precondition for trust in all cases. There is honor even among thieves. Those who violate the code, whatever it may be, are ostracized. In societies where ethical standards are higher, lying, cheating, stealing, and other violations of the code must be dealt with swiftly and surely in order that the climate of trust be preserved.

Trust Defined

"Trust is the belief or confidence in the honesty, integrity, reliability and justice of another person or thing." This definition from *Webster's* suits the purpose of this book, although it does not address the distinctions that are offered in the Random House definition of trust, which differentiates among trust, confidence, and assurance. In the Random House version, trust implies instinctive, unquestioning belief; confidence implies conscious trust because of good reasons; and assurance implies absolute confidence and certainty. In my view, these nuances need not be absolute demarcations. Rather, they can be on a continuum. Moreover, they are situational. For instance, an ingenuous propensity to trust is often reciprocated and can serve to bring out the best in others. Stories abound in history, literature, and folklore about Jean Valjeans and potential miscreants who have turned around because someone trusted them. Similarly, the stories of battlefield heroes and other unusual achievers make us realize that we often underestimate the selflessness of others. The basic propensity to trust, in these respects, is both virtuous and pragmatic. Carried too far, it is foolhardy. Trusting one's life with a quack just because he says he is a skilled surgeon is reckless. Walking into the proverbial den of thieves, unarmed physically and mentally, is quixotic. Trusting a stranger to perform a crucial task when a tried and tempered colleague is available is grist for a movie plot but can be the script for a tragedy. In these respects, trust is also provisional—it must be earned.

Aim, Vision, Mission, Values, Objectives, and Goals

Trust is easier to achieve when the enterprise's sense of purpose is both understood and shared by the organization and its people. Not all need be in lock step. Nor does the individual need to be submerged in "group-think." There is plenty of room for diversity and individual initiative in pursuit of the purpose. But if the sense of purpose is either not understood or if irreconcilable differences about the end (not the means) exist, a trusting environment is difficult to achieve.

The hierarchy implied by the terminology—aim, vision, mission, values, objectives, and goals—leaves plenty of room for diversity and individual interpretation. If the aim is the improvement of society, the umbrella is big enough for Democrats, Republicans, Libertarians, and Socialists. As one travels down the hierarchy, this umbrella becomes smaller; nevertheless, the methods of achievement are usually richly diverse. Even when they are not, the sharing of effort to achieve an agreed-upon outcome engenders trust.

But when there are serious differences about the purposes or the method of achievement, or when the method of measuring and rewarding success creates disharmony, trust is at risk. Similarly, when there is no sense of purpose, when the members of the orchestra are all playing from different scores, harmony becomes discord, and the opportunity for trust is diminished.

The Roots of Mistrust in Organizations

The roots of mistrust in organizations are (1) the misalignment of measurements and rewards, (2) incompetence or the presumption of incompetence, (3) lack of appreciation for a system, (4) untrustworthy information, and (5) integrity failure. (See Figure 1.) These five causes, like components of a system, are also intertwined. Therefore, they will not be addressed serially but will serve as an underlying diagnostic framework for most of the book's issues. Some, like the misalignment of measurements and rewards, and incompetence and its presumption, are more pervasive than others—and will merit separate chapter headings—but all the causes are usually involved in major failures of trust. Although the causes of mistrust are essentially interwoven and

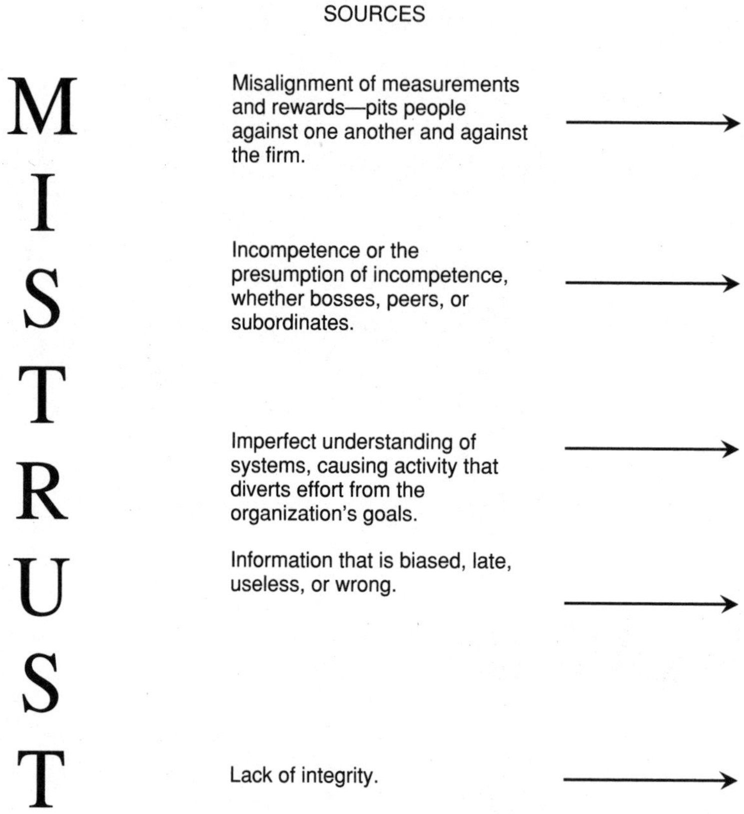

SOURCES

M

I   Misalignment of measurements
           and rewards—pits people   ⟶
           against one another and against
           the firm.

S

           Incompetence or the
           presumption of incompetence,   ⟶
T   whether bosses, peers, or
           subordinates.

R   Imperfect understanding of   ⟶
           systems, causing activity that
           diverts effort from the
           organization's goals.

           Information that is biased, late,
U   useless, or wrong.   ⟶

S

           Lack of integrity.   ⟶
T

Figure 1.

FACTORS

⟶ Establish the aim, mission, vision, and values of the firm, then manage as an inclusive system—rewarding the whole human being in a way that also rewards the firm.

⟶ Create a permeable organization structure and interactive management processes in an open, trusting environment—for learning on the job and as multiplier of formal training and education.

⟶ Understand and communicate the interdependence of all components.

⟶ Conduct an audit of formal and informal measurements and controls. Eliminate noise— defined as information that does not contribute to the central mission of the firm, which is to profitably design, build, and sell a product or service.

⟶ Remove violators from the system, swiftly and summarily. Eliminate conditions that might cause recurrence.

T
R
U
S
T

addressed in different forms throughout the book, they do require some amount of individual discussion.

1. *Misalignment of measurements and rewards.* Sometimes we ask people to do one thing but measure them on something else that is either peripheral or dysfunctional to the objective. Thus one large and formerly respected company addressed its troubled state by decreeing that 10 percent of each work unit would be eliminated by the end of the year. In a triumph of human resource department reasoning, the company also decreed that one of the criteria for selection of survivors is "teamwork."

Sometimes rewards for one activity negatively affect another: the salesman receives a big bonus for exceeding quota, but production and distribution people have negative variances because of unplanned overtime that is required to ship his orders. Or we pay managers based on the number of people they supervise, yet we exhort them to reduce head count.

Examples are legion and distressingly familiar to managers whom I come in contact with. Many of them just shake their heads and do the best they can. But the consequences are not less benign than the managers' dispirited resignation might suggest. These misalignments create intolerable waste and complexity. They pit people against each other and against the firm. More important, the misalignments prompt organizational narcissism and detract from the organization's real purpose—getting and keeping profitable customers.

2. *Incompetence or the presumption of incompetence.* This is perhaps the most costly of all the causes. We hire people who lack the requisite knowledge or skills. Then, instead of helping them correct their deficiencies, we supervise and inspect them. The cost is enormous considering the layers of supervision and the concomitant suboptimization that springs from a dispirited work force that is doing what it is told under the watchful eyes of bosses. In other instances we just assume that people are incompetent without giving them a real chance to show what they can do. If we are lucky, these people will channel their untapped potential to extracurricular activities. If we are unlucky, we will pay the price when their latent or overt anger is directed to the workplace.

Competence applies to organizations as well as to people. Organizational structures and processes play a profound role in the success of the enterprise. The permeable organization structure and interactive processes in an open, trusting environment provide the enterprise with pertinent and timely information and the ability to properly assess the external environment. Furthermore, such a structure helps to mobilize the firm's internal resources so the company can not only react but lead. Business leaders who know how to develop and mobilize the competence of individuals and the enterprise will always prevail over the hidebound bureaucratic firm. As several sobered CEOs of the *Fortune* 500 can attest, a strong balance sheet is about as permanent as the snows of yesteryear when the firm has lost its competence to read, react, or lead.

3. *Lack of appreciation of a system.* Some managers do not fully appreciate the aphorism, "A chain is as strong as its weakest link." A customer's receiving clerk might be the deciding factor in a decision to change suppliers. The design of the product could be brilliant, the manufacturing nearly perfect, but if the shipping department misdirects the product, packs it poorly, ships it late, or chooses an unreliable carrier, the firm's design and excellent manufacturing could be rendered meaningless if the customer's receiving clerk has the ears of the decision makers. Similarly, a customer's accounts-payable manager could make the difference in a close call between two suppliers. If the billing is consistently late, confusing, or wrong, the relationship is at risk.

The weak links in a production chain are sometimes more visible than those in support functions and therefore are more apt to be improved. But business is more than production. Value should be added at each step, from conception to payment. If the sales force is poorly trained, if order entry and customer service functions are ineffective, if the telephone operator is rude, if the producer does not fully utilize the skills of the firm's suppliers, if customer needs are assessed incorrectly, then the company could be the victim of Peter Drucker's poignant observation, "There is nothing worse than doing the wrong thing well."

The moral: No part of a system is more important than another. Some functions may require greater skill, harder or more dangerous work; but each part must do its job. The challenge to leaders is to understand fully the system they are managing, to understand the interdependence of the various components, to spend their creative energy improving the interface between the components as well as improving the components themselves.

A leader must do more than react to the most recent data point, whether it is a production report or a financial statement. Leaders must understand the capabilities of all the components of the system then work to improve the components, not on their own terms alone but via how the components contribute to the systems that the leaders manage. If leaders do not understand the system, they will not know what or whom to trust. And if a leader's ignorance of the system is apparent to the people who work in it, they will not trust her or him.

4. *Untrustworthy information.* When information that managers are expected to act on is incomplete, biased, or wrong, trust is always at risk. Untrustworthy information produces defensive mechanisms, which add to the cycle of mistrust and its inevitable cost to the enterprise. Here is an example from a firm that I work with. One of its product lines that produces 20 percent of its revenues reports an appropriate cost of goods. Traditional accounting practice shows that the product is profitable. But a few inquiries indicated that 80 percent of the selling and administrative costs were driven by this seemingly profitable line that produced only 20 percent of the revenues. These managers had been uneasy about the line's profitability, but the monthly financial reports created a schizophrenia that was not resolved until all the costs had been identified.

Recently, I talked to a manager who had received a long memorandum from an associate. I asked him what went through his mind as he read it. His response: "Before I even read the report, I looked to see who received copies—then I wondered who received the blind copies. Only then did I read the report, and when I read it, I was trying to figure out his angle." Does this sound like the stuff that great companies are made of? Fortuitously, some companies are good in spite of this kind of wasted energy. Imagine how great they could be if mistrust had not been fostered by untrustworthy information!

Managers are expected to react to the products of the financial alphabet—NPV, DCF, ROI, ROA, ROAE, PAT, EBIT, EBITDA—yet intuitively they know that ratios tell only a part of the story—that an uncritical reaction to ratios will often lead them astray. I tell my students that the most profound thing that I will ever teach them is that every ratio has a numerator and a denominator—and that a rich understanding of this verity will change their lives.

Earlier I mentioned the problem with adversarial behavior and the potential problems of advocacy. It is a travesty that managers must spend more time trying to figure out what was not in a report than they do in understanding the words it contains. The examples are ubiquitous and costly, not only in terms of wasted time but also in bad decisions and misdirected efforts.

5. *Failure of integrity.*   I am speaking of overt failure—lying, cheating, stealing. If trust is to play any part in the enterprise, these must be dealt with swiftly and summarily. The transgressor must be removed from the enterprise. If integrity failure is overlooked anywhere, trust will be tarnished everywhere. Fortunately, the costs from failure of integrity are not as prevalent as those from the other four causes; but when failure of integrity does occur, it cannot be ignored.

Mistrust and Downsizing

As I write this, our society faces a conundrum. Present economic indicators are encouraging, but the same factors that may be contributing to economic recovery are fostering continued high unemployment. Productivity improvements are coming out of the hides of managers, staff specialists, and hourly workers. Their unemployment, in turn, damps the rate of recovery.

Business cycle forecasters were late to recognize that U.S. economic problems, even in the 1970s and early 1980s, were structural as well as cyclical. Too many people were doing too little productive work. Costs were too high. Ability to innovate was diminished. Some markets were lost to competition; other markets shrank significantly. Because we did not know how to recapture our markets, we have, since the late 1970s, had to downsize, right-size, de-layer, rationalize—all pseudonyms for firing people. This activity intensified in the early 1990s. It probably will continue for the foreseeable future as companies that cannot compete on terms of cost, quality, and time are forced to restructure in order to play in the same leagues with firms that have previously streamlined their operations.

Here are four of the factors that contributed to our problems by driving our costs up and dulling our market senses. First, the management methods, policies, and procedures that seemed appropriate for controlling post–World War II growth spawned a costly hierarchy and administrative bureaucracy that stultified the productive potential of managers and workers. Competitors, particularly those from the Pacific Rim, managed their businesses more efficiently and effectively. We lost our edge.

Second, some businesses, in efforts to defend their own markets, have instigated and supported protectionist laws, regulations, taxes, and tariffs. Competitors, domestic and offshore, quite naturally retaliated by sponsoring their own forms of protection. Now, both sides as well as the economy in general are tangled up in red tape.

Third, when businesses could not find someone to regulate, our public servants could. Perhaps their dealings with special interests had exposed them only to the seamy side of business. In any event, they found the key to guaranteed employment. Their primary purpose now seems to be to tax, regulate, and control, not to encourage growth.

Fourth, the trade union movement also contributed to our plight. Crippling work rules and prohibitions on productivity improvement from technology made us sitting ducks for competitors with less hampered work forces.

Now, before those of different economic or political persuasions throw down this book in disgust, let me acknowledge that business got the unions it deserved, that some regulations are necessary, that health costs are also a drag on productivity, and that low wages and disregard of the environment in some of our competitors' countries have contributed to their short-term competitive advantage. Let me acknowledge also that other industrial societies have imposed onerous constraints on business, although some, along with the newly industrialized societies, have supported their business enterprises. On balance, however, the distinct competitive advantage we once held has evaporated. We seem to have forgotten that business is the engine of our society. Rather than throw sand in the crankcase, we should look for the oil can.

What does all this have to do with downsizing and mistrust? Because the regulatory momentum is so great, business has had to concentrate efforts on areas over which it has the greatest influence—its own management methods, practices, and policies, and its own work force, both organized and unorganized.

Accordingly, since the late 1970s business has been downsizing with concomitant improvements in traditional productivity measures. Indeed, by the early 1990s productivity of U.S. industry was as good or better than other industrialized countries. Some of these gains came because we were working smarter as well as working harder. We were producing more goods and services with fewer people.

When we laid off people during periods of economic growth, the pain, great as it was, was ameliorated because most of those who were terminated could quickly find other employment. However, during the late 1980s and early 1990s, the economy has been relatively stagnant. The pain has increased greatly.

The implications have not escaped present survivors of business purges. Managers and employees are afraid—and rightly so. Their fear may motivate effort, but it undermines further change. Understandably, they want to preserve the status quo. They are not persuaded by the story about the castaways crowded on a lifeboat. Someone in the bow admonished, "Don't rock the boat." Whereupon a voice from the stern called out, "Yes, just keep it level while it sinks."

It is in this environment that a turnaround manager turned college professor asks you to consider trust as a lever to pry out waste and unnecessary complexity, trust as a liberator of the organization's latent creative energy. To the extent that people in the organization suspect that they will be considered waste and complexity, they fear that the liberation will be *from* their jobs—not *in* their jobs.

Nevertheless, waste and complexity must go if a company is to compete successfully with the so-called world-class companies. Moreover, it needs to realize the true potential of the people in the business enterprise if it plans to play a significant role in the world economic order. Reestablishing trust in this unsettled environment will test the skill and resolve of business leaders. The task is not impossible, however; if the surviving employees and managers understand that the previous downsizing activities were indeed necessary, if they believe that those who were terminated were treated fairly, if they see that remaining managers are sharing the pain, and if they believe that the business is on the right course to recovery,[1] they will put forth their best efforts. As I have stated before, the successful operational turnaround is a useful model. Once the agonizing days of terminations are over—under proper leadership—trust and its benefits are nearly always realized.

Unfortunately, there is no satisfactory answer for those qualified people who have lost and will lose their jobs. They are paying the price for our past practices, for our arrogance, and for our unwillingness to change—even after the need was recognized. Unemployment and underemployment of qualified men and women could indeed be a problem through the 1990s. There will be more layoffs, more terminations. Some of the giant companies that moved too slowly now have few other realistic options. Moreover, if one company in an industry has streamlined itself effectively, others will have to follow suit if they are to remain competitive.

But, far too often, businesses have handled downsizing clumsily. They have fired the wrong people for the wrong reasons and have not removed waste and unnecessary complexity, with the result that the survivors' work load was massive and unfocused. Moreover, using people as ballast that can be added or discarded every time a squall appears on the horizon is not only inhumane, it is bad business. When the clouds gather and personal survival is at stake, no one will pay proper attention to the aims of the enterprise. Several industrial giants have blundered seriously by using what my colleague Robert Lear calls "the salami technique" of downsizing. People in these organizations were paralyzed, wondering if they would be the next slice. Their paralysis accelerated the spiral; their reduced effectiveness fed the need for even more and deeper cuts.

When downsizing is the only realistic answer, it should be strategic as well as tactical. Moreover, people should be seen as assets, not costs. Finally, a business cannot take the people out if it does not take the work out. Let's look at these in turn:

First, the strategic aspect of downsizing implies that the firm knows what it wants to do now and in the future. Toward that end, the firm makes sure that it identifies and preserves the core competencies that are required to meet its strategic goals.

Second, when people are recognized as assets, the firm makes certain that the people who are required for the execution of the core competencies are not only kept in place but are not subjected to paralyzing fear.

Finally, when people are removed from any business operation, a corresponding amount of work should be removed. Only rarely are people in organizations so idle that the survivors can continue to perform adequately unless some tasks are discontinued—unless waste and complexity are removed. Otherwise, important work will fall between the cracks, the people will burn out, and ultimately the organization will fail or warp back into its former shape.

There could be a silver lining to all this gloom. My earlier forecast of severe dislocations from downsizing need not be realized. I am not Malthusian, nor a member of the Club of Rome. Even with all the world's problems and terrible tragedies, it is a better place today than it was yesterday, and it can be a better place tomorrow. Even with inequities and delays, improved living standards in one society tend to improve standards in others. But this requires political and social policy that resists the foolish attempt to lift the general welfare by pulling down its leading economic producers. Regression to the mean in this manner lowers the mean and does not necessarily narrow the distribution.

Similarly, successful companies have the responsibility to grow ethically. Moreover, their modus operandi should reject growth by trampling on the competition. Rather, growth should come from serving the economic needs of society, by keeping a clear, crisp focus on customers. In these respects, Schumpeter's creative destruction is a useful concept for excising the firm's outmoded practices, policies, and procedures to make way for the new, but it does not license the destruction of one business by another. The ebb and flow of success and failure are outcomes, not objectives.

On the microecomonic level, businesses can avoid severe dislocation if their leaders can unlearn the old aphorism, "Take care of the present and the future will take care of itself." The leader's job *is* the future. Certainly, business leaders need to create organizations that can take care of the present. But when the leader forgets the future, innovation suffers, and waste and unnecessary complexity—those brothers and sisters of bureaucracy—take over. The business stagnates. Competitors grow strong in existing markets and stake strong claims in new markets. The approaching crisis is inexorable, but often invisible to the complacent leader. Then when the crisis can no longer be ignored, the dislocations begin. Downsizing and restructuring with a vengeance! A needless waste! The business with its eye on the future restructures itself every day. Dislocation is replaced with innovation, as well as with constant and orderly change. The jobs of people change, but business has prepared the way. Cross-training, assignment rotation, constant attention to new ideas and improved technologies will help lift the business to new levels where job creation replaces job destruction.

Ensuring the future and its attendant hope for a brighter employment picture will require a high degree of trust—trust that people can do their jobs without excessive supervision, trust that they are inclined and motivated to focus on the customer instead of adversarial activities and bureaucratic ploys that enervate organizational vitality. But trust is reciprocal. Business cannot expect to trust when it condones or rewards the causes of mistrust. The five causes that were identified earlier—misalignment of measurements and rewards, incompetence or the presumption of incompetence, lack of appreciation for systems, untrustworthy information, and lack of integrity—are not always separable. They are interwoven in each chapter; however, in the interest of structure, Part 1 of this book will focus primarily on systems, rewards, information, and integrity; and Part 2 will investigate the relationship of trust to organizational and individual competence.

PART 1

Rewards, Measurements, and Controls

- Some jobs are more demanding than others.
- Some people are demonstrably better at their jobs than others.
- The marketplace rates the job and the person.

It follows, then:

- Some people will be paid more than others.

Attempts to repeal the market paradigm above would be folly. But just as fall acious is the attempt to measure with implied precision the difficulty of the job or the ability of the person. There are too many variables. The permutations are infinite. Moreover, the attempt to measure the job or the person as if they were independent of the system in which they operate is impossible. Yet we have created an expensive army of professionals whose methods imply that those variables can be measured precisely over relatively short terms. Costly as it is, this army's direct expense is dwarfed by the costs it loads on the enterprise. Some of these are: managers and employees, enacting the annual merit review rituals; managers determining whether someone's merit raise should be 4.3 percent or 4.5 percent, or whose incentive bonus should be 10 percent of base pay or 12 percent. In most instances, these well-meaning efforts to motivate have the opposite effect.

The cruelest cost, however, might well be the signal that money is all that matters. We acknowledge the importance of the whole human being, but we spend so much creative energy devising pay plans that we minimize other compensation factors. In addition, many of our attempts to reward people damage the firm. Any reward system that does not also adequately reward the firm will ultimately reward no one.

The next five chapters will address the complex and vexing problems of rewards, measurements, and controls. These chapters will not offer prescriptions but will propose a theoretical basis which will allow the enterprise to address its specific needs in its own way.

3

Walking Our Talk: Realignment of Measurements and Rewards

A business is a system of complex activities conducted within interdependent functions. Yet its numeric measurements carry the presumption that the activities are simple; its reward systems generally reflect the presumption that the functions stand alone. Then both are confounded by the presumption that measurements should determine rewards. These misalignments diminish trust in both our measurements and in each other.

In response, we make adjustments. To deal with measurement problems, we develop new indexes or design new reports. To deal with problems of people, we design new incentive programs. We change the annual merit review forms. In extreme cases we reorganize. But the problems do not go away. So we try again. And again. As the spiral widens and deepens, we discover that we are spending more time and energy on administering measurements and rewards than on the real work of the firm, which is designing, producing, selling, distributing, and collecting for a product or service that will get and keep profitable customers.

Why are we in this spiral? We are tinkering with symptoms, not dealing with causes. We are measuring outcomes but ignoring the process. Furthermore, business processes cannot be measured with numbers alone, and the most important losses and gains defy measurement of any kind.[1] Complex activities that *can* be measured cannot be measured with a single numeric indicator, not even a ratio. Especially not a ratio!

One function cannot be measured as if it were independent of others. It is not. Nor can people be measured as if they are independent of their colleagues. They are not. Furthermore, there is always variation in the things that we measure. When we take action without understanding what variation is trying to tell us, we often make things worse.

Until we understand variation, and until we realign measurements and rewards to conform to the way work is done, we will continue to fritter away time. Worse, because many of our reward systems are zero sum, we will continue to pit people against each other, losing the benefit of their creative cooperation. Even worse, because the reward system seems unfair, we will continue to pit people against the firm. In too many instances, the company has become the enemy: "Every man for himself." Let's be honest: "To hell with all of them" is a phrase I have heard more than once. Whether the fault is with the employee or with the firm is not the central issue. Where this adversarial attitude is pervasive, the loss is incalculable. Admittedly, employee priorities cannot be exactly congruent with those of the firm. But they should be parallel.

Until we realign the measurement and reward system, we will forgo the full potential of the new quality and productivity enhancement methods, nearly all of which cut across functions on the traditional organization chart. But our present measurement and reward system is tied to the traditional functional form. How do we realign a measurement system to properly evaluate quick response systems, self-directed work groups, time compression, reengineering, simultaneous engineering, fast-track construction, process management, and a host of other promising cross-functional breakthroughs?

In short, how do we reward a system of interdependent parts? The answer is simple: We reward the system, not the parts. But if we continue with our traditional measurements and rewards of individuals as if they were independent, then functional isolationism will contribute to the further decline of our relative productivity. Our quality will lag behind. As a result, our ability to compete will continue to wither.

These are serious charges and require substantiation. To that end, I will first address situations where measurements and rewards are closely linked but misaligned.

Rewards Confounded by Measurements

In reality, every business reward is confounded by measurements. Hard as we try, we cannot isolate the key variables in order to have confidence in cause and effect. "But," you may respond, "what about the saleswoman who exceeds her target? She is dependent only on her own hard work." Well, let's control for the variable "hard work." Consider the following questions and observations: "Was the target fair?" Like a canny golfer who negotiates a handicap on the first tee, some salespeople win their bonuses at budget time. "Was there an unexpected windfall?" One response could be: "So what? Windfalls and downturns even out over time." Perhaps they do. Nevertheless, their existence confirms the hypothesis. Windfalls and downturns are neither direct causes nor effects of her hard work. "Did she borrow from next period's sales to make her target?" Worse, did she say to the customer, "Let me ship it. You can always send it back." The total cost of processing and handling a return for most products exceeds their sale price. Not for the Kohinoor diamond, no! But for components or products which sell for less than $100, usually yes! Moreover, her gain is the distribution center's loss. Ask distribution managers who are measured in units, pounds, or tons shipped how they feel about the paperwork and the warehouse labor hours to unpack, inspect, and restock returned merchandise. How does this contribute to their trust that they are being fairly compensated? Less onerous but still costly is the unplanned overtime required for the distribution manager to get the goods out the door just before the month, quarter, or year end. The sales manager made her bonus but wiped out the chances for a bonus in distribution.

None of these observations is intended to excuse laziness or wrong-headedness on the saleswoman's part. She should be expected to do her job. But if motivated and managed properly, she can make more money for herself and the firm and she can have greater job security than she can by spending time and creative energy playing the numbers games.

Now let's tinker with the process. Let's set monthly sales quotas as a target for a fixed monthly bonus. Fine! Now the saleswoman who makes the big sale early in the period can go to the movies or can postpone orders in order to provide a cushion for next period. Is this in the best interest of the firm? Perhaps we should adjust the incentive plan again. How would you adjust it? Would you pay on a sliding scale with no limits? Would you measure it weekly? Monthly? Semiannually? How would you deal with returns and uncollected accounts receivable? Would you expect the saleswoman to assess the creditworthiness of her customers? If not, how would you adjudicate the arguments between the credit manager and the saleswoman?

Among other issues, the foregoing raise the question: "Is the unit of time appropriate for the measurement?" More "chance and fortune" is associated with daily results than with ten years' sales performance. Indeed, this observation presages one of the recommendations for improvement in our reward and measurement systems: use of longer periods of time before important decisions. Even then, however, the variables are complexly related, making it difficult to determine cause and effect. In the early 1980s, would Apple Computer's sales manager have been as successful had he been selling Sinclair Computers?

The question is: How do you measure success? To whom can you compare your sales manager for purposes of devising an incentive plan? Although no salespeople would admit it publicly, some products almost sell themselves—until the competition comes out with a product that eclipses theirs. Then, as any salesperson would say, "No one can sell that dog. I'm going to look for another job." How do you respond to the old bromide in the beer business, "It was either lousy weather or a great salesperson." Let's confound it further. I was once in the advertising business. For our soft drink client it was much the same: "Lousy weather if the sales were bad, great advertising if the sales were good." The salesperson was irrelevant.

Certainly, some salespeople are better than others. Some work harder, have better communication skills, greater empathy, a sixth sense about when to close. But this cannot be determined by isolated sales results alone. It is determined also by close observation over time in different conditions with different customer targets. Numbers alone are insufficient to determine whether the numbers were a result of skill or luck.

Anecdotes about the games that salespeople play are usually livelier than for more mundane activities. But the problem is pervasive and deadly serious. I have seen a publishing company at the brink of bankruptcy because the CEO who was measured and rewarded by the bottom line naively printed too many copies of each title in order to bring down the unit cost of goods. He reported a profit but ran out of cash. For some titles, he had enough books to support sales for 20 years.

I have seen a manufacturing company brought to its knees by the same game. The manufacturing VP and the CEO were willing, naive conspirators. As units produced went up, average cost per unit went down. The manufacturing VP made his productivity bonus, and the CEO made his profit target, because the cost of goods per unit went down and the gross margin went up. But the distribution center was bulging. Extra warehouses were rented. The company ran out of cash. But until problems were revealed, the company reported profitable operations, and the officers got their bonuses. Indeed, in many of the biggest bankruptcies of the last decade, the independent auditors had given a "clean" opinion in the fiscal year preceding the bankruptcy. This is not to blame or absolve the auditors, it is to reiterate the shortcomings of numerical measures and traditional financial reporting; it is to dramatize the problem with reward and incentive systems which do not—often cannot—reflect the complexities of the activities that they reward. Ironically, this seems to support arguments made by defenders of the present system. "The system is not wrong, it is the people that manipulate the system for their own gain." There is some merit to this response, as we shall see later; however, the anecdotes from the most respected U.S.

companies, as well as companies in crisis, are not isolated—they are universal. Isn't it about time for us to admit that there may be something wrong with the system? That we cannot measure complex systems as if they are simple, that we cannot properly measure them with numbers alone?

Let's look at two more examples; these are from retailing and distribution. Recently I assisted a supermarket chain in restructure of its organization. The first activity was to conduct a throughput study, starting with the customer and then working upstream. Interviews with customers indicated satisfaction with the shopping experience, with an important exception: They reported that they could not find some of the staple grocery and household items on weekends. One woman reported that the store was out of stock on 64-oz. boxes of Tide. Perplexing! Stores never run out of Tide! "If you're out of Tide, you're out of business!" Customers will shift to stores that can provide their staple needs.

Proceeding upstream, I then interviewed the store managers who reported that many other items they were ordering from the central distribution center were not being shipped in time for weekend business. Not only were they running out of merchandise, they were having serious trouble with their labor scheduling. They did not have enough personnel for stocking shelves early in the week and had too many on the weekend! By the time I moved upstream to the distribution center, I had formed a hypothesis that received partial confirmation from their complaints. Whereas trucks that delivered merchandise to the distribution center for reshipment to the stores were lined up for blocks on Wednesday, Thursday, and Friday, Monday and Tuesday deliveries trickled to almost nothing. The reason for this was that merchandise unloaded during the last half of the week was first held in the staging area until workers had time later to put it in the slots for selection and shipment to the stores. This double handling caused by the glut of late-week receivings and other schedule disruptions had ruined the chance for distribution center managers who were rewarded with incentive bonuses on the number of units shipped per labor hour. They were livid.

Now I was sure I knew the culprit. When I arrived at the purchasing department I found that in the company's attempt to manage cash, the buyers were being measured on the warehouse inventory turns of the products that they were responsible for. The day the turns were measured was Tuesday. If on Tuesdays the warehouses held full stocks of the products that the buyers were responsible for, the buyers would miss out on that week's incentive plan. The buyers were not dummies. They called suppliers and threatened to break their knees if trucks showed up on Monday or Tuesday. The buyers got their bonuses. The customer did not get her Tide.

The Profit Center Fallacy

There is only one true profit center in a company. That is the company itself. All else is confounded by allocation of resources, transfer pricing, overhead spreading, and other accounting fictions. Moreover, the quest for so-called profits in a profit center usually suboptimizes the profits of the firm. I acknowledge that the famed Asea Brown Boveri Company is flourishing with 5000 profit centers, and that many firms have used the profit center concept to substantially reduce the size of central administration. Profit center companies that are successful in the long run are not successful just because they use profit centers but because of highly interactive management processes. Moreover, I am not critical of the attempt to determine which divisions, products, or customers make a contribution to profits. On the contrary, information like this is crucial to a firm's success. But when the profits are deemed to be determinable independently of the corporate allocation decisions or other uncontrollable factors, and when people are measured and rewarded on the basis of the so-called profit plans alone, gamesmanship overtakes the serious work of the firm.

For example, the profit center concept helped to bring the mighty General Motors to its knees. Division profits, adjusted by transfer pricing and allocation decisions, were duly reported. In addition, executives were rewarded on the basis of sales and sales increases. Because bonuses and promotions were at stake, executives in one division did not want to be eclipsed by another, so each division set out to build a full line, with these unintended results: blurring of any clear image lines may once have had and duplication of costs. A marketing strategist might opine that this proliferation of models was the appropriate response to an increasing diversity among consumers. After all, Henry Ford is gone. The black Model T strategy has been supplanted by niche marketing. I have been told, however, that this model proliferation was not strategy, but a "happening." In their quest for sales, General Motors divisional executives ignored the complaints of customers that "This really is not an Oldsmobile—it has a Chevrolet engine, a Buick frame, and an Oldsmobile decal." They ignored the derision of industry observers when Cadillac brought out the Cimarron, which one friend of mine characterized as a Chevrolet with leather seats. The Cimarron has been given a decent burial, and the Cadillac division now seems on a clearer course, but the GM model spectrum still is mind-boggling.

The cost differential is staggering. Dr. Deming has been told by a GM executive that this structural differential accounts for $200 of the $795 unit cost differential (1990) between General Motors and Ford.

The distribution center at a large supermarket chain was called a profit center, and its managers received bonuses in relationship to its reported profitability. The distribution center's revenue came from a so-called upcharge—a percentage added to the wholesale value of the merchandise it shipped. In 1971 and 1972, the distribution center struggled to make money. In some instances its managers postponed maintenance of equipment in order to make any profit at all. Then in 1973, they began to report almost unbelievable improvement. The managers swaggered into the monthly financial reviews, lording it over the other executives who were reporting some improvement but nothing compared with the distribution center. The beneficiaries of the big distribution center bonuses lamely explained their success as "good management." Someone else had to call to their attention—and the company's—that food inflation in 1973 was around 13 percent. Their percentage upcharge meant that they were receiving a 13 percent increase in revenue for handling the same amount of merchandise. And it all dropped to the bottom line! Their "success," in addition to being ephemeral, also lulled the managers into laxity on achievement of real gains in productivity.

These same luminaries fought for productivity and profits by insisting that everything possible be shipped through the distribution center. Twenty-one of the supermarket chain's stores were in Long Island, and five or six of their stores were located in southern New Jersey, both of which are premium growing areas for fresh fruits and vegetables. In keeping with distribution center policy, sweet corn was picked, loaded on open trucks, transported to the distribution center, where it was then shipped back to the stores that were on the original route of the farmers' trucks. Long Island potatoes trundled past 21 of the Long Island stores to the warehouse in central New Jersey, then right back to the same stores. Green beans, tomatoes, lettuce, celery, broccoli all made the fateful round trips. These products are not fine wines—they do not improve with age. By the time they made it from the distribution center back to the stores, they had lost much of their flavor, nutrition, and appearance. But they had gained something very important—the upcharge. Formidable! Wilted *and* expensive! And the supermarket chain wondered why it had a poor reputation for fresh produce.

The distribution center managers defended their actions in the name of quality. They had to inspect it at the distribution center to maintain quality standards. Along the way they gained two powerful allies—the finance department, which said that bookkeeping for direct store delivery of perishable items during the summer season was too complex, and the audit department, which said that the managers of the store could not be trusted— managers might solicit kickbacks from the farmers.

The quality objection was easy to answer: Training, if needed. However, most of the managers of store produce knew as much about quality as the distribution center inspectors. The next objection was like the tail wagging the dog. Installation of accounting procedures was an insignificant problem compared with the opportunity to sell fresher merchandise at lower prices. But the accountants were at headquarters, close to the seat of power. The produce managers were too far away to be seen or heard. The third objection had merit insofar as there probably were some managers who would solicit or take kickbacks. This type of transgression should be dealt with summarily and harshly but should not be allowed to spoil the system. Whatever the reason, the decision to sell stale merchandise at higher prices dramatizes the economics of trust. Moreover, in this case, the losses were much greater than those attributable to the produce items themselves. Supermarket customers usually go where they can get the best value on perishable items as well as canned goods and household items. In this case, they voted with their feet. They went to smaller stores with less sophisticated accounting systems who bought the produce directly from growers in the area. The company's total loss in this instance is again incalculable.

Of course, not all cost differentials are attributable to profit centers, but certainly the managerial staffing levels and duplication of facilities are major contributors, unless they too are controlled. The cost of politicization of decision making is more difficult to measure but is enormous.

But the biggest losses can stem from an ineffective strategy. When strategy abdicates to numbers produced by profit centers, the enterprise usually loses its focus. Product strategy is the responsibility of the most senior leaders, who look at the enterprise as a whole, then make the tough resource allocation decisions, regardless of reported short-term profits and regardless of the protestations of clamoring fiefdoms. Indeed, when the system is managed properly, there will be no fiefdoms. Everyone will be marching to the same song. Profits to the firm will soar.

Bankers have destroyed themselves by almost every method except self-immolation. One of their more destructive innovations was to measure and reward lending departments as profit centers. And in order to be exactly wrong, they measured results monthly, quarterly, and annually. Moreover, revenues were measured not only by income from interest, but also by fees, points, discounts, and other devices which were considered income when the loan was put on the books. The "income" was not spread over the life of the loan. Furthermore, they measured "income," not "net losses of income." Of course, it is difficult to measure losses early. Even if the loan starts to sour, bankers sweeten it by relaxing covenants, and in some instances by lending more money so the borrower can made payments on past-due interest or principal—sometimes both. If Lewis Carroll had lived today, the setting for *Alice in Wonderland* would have been a big commercial bank. Stories are legion about bank presidents and other senior officers who made some of the banks' worst loans. Fortunately for them, they had been promoted away from their problems. Why? Their profit centers had achieved their targets. Were profit centers the only reason bankers are in trouble? Of course not. Some of the seven deadly sins also were prime movers—the profit centers were the facilitators.

There is an ironic postscript to this story. In the early 1990s, most banks were in such disarray that they could no longer make what once would have been considered sound commercial loans, once the life blood of their business. Moreover, when an existing borrower, or industry, sails into even mildly troubled waters, the banks run for the harbor. When it is time to renew the loan, or if the company has even a small technical violation, the banks will say, "We will rest our line," a euphemism for "You're not getting any more money, and worse: Pay us back now!" The once valued concept of relationship banking built on mutual trust has almost disappeared. Banks in 1993 are returning to profitability. Perhaps they will return to lending.

Charles Darwin and the Incentive Pay Fallacy

We do not need Charles Darwin to tell us that meat-eaters eat meat, and that the swifter, stronger, smarter, eat the others. Nor do we need him to tell us that the offspring of the stronger are more apt to prevail than offspring of the weaker. Pray that we do not need him to tell us that the foregoing is not an appropriate or realistic model for economic enterprise either within the firm or external to it!

Attack-response theorists and economists with black boxes in a frictionless world seem to believe that businesses prosper by feeding on the carcasses of others. Successful business people know that prosperity comes not from killing and scavenging but from intense and unwavering focus on needs of customers. Obviously, the company that stays ahead of the needs of customers will prosper while others will not, but that is an outcome, not an objective. Similarly, only personnel managers who use numeric scales for grading people, or line managers who "force-rank" their subordinates, believe in the zero-sum game of winners and losers which kills off or maims the productive potential of the greatest part of their population.

Corrupted Darwinism

Darwin's survival of the fittest was not meant to advocate a killing field but to show us how species adapt so that they can survive in a changing, sometimes hostile environment. Over time, some make it. Others don't. Again—an outcome in nature, not the objective in business. Moreover, Darwin acknowledged that a species cannot survive alone. It needs others, not as much for food as to produce an ecosystem which nourishes all.

Unfortunately, the underlying assumptions of many of our management practices are a corruption of Darwin's magnificent contribution. Business is not, nor need it be, zero sum: for every winner a loser, kill or be killed, make progress only by climbing over the backs of others! Admittedly, these phrases overstate general practice, but they are all phrases I have heard in the halls and offices of U.S. businesses. "Dog eat dog" is another phrase I often hear, not necessarily to criticize the system but to describe it—sometimes, to justify it. "Give them some resources, then stand aside and watch. The strong will survive to run the company in the future, the others will fall by the way." Hardly conducive to trust. Only the predators will really wish to come to work in the morning. The others, who would rather be safely at home, will spend their time looking for trees to climb or crevices to hide in. Wasted effort, if the job of business is to design, finance, build, sell, and collect for a product or service!

Nevertheless, elements of this corrupted Darwinism are beguiling and sometimes seem to be supported. Common sense and simple observation confirm that people perform some tasks well and other tasks poorly. Some do most things well. Others do most things poorly. So, let them fight it out, reward the winners, and bury the losers.

What is lost in this line of reasoning is that not all people do the *same* thing well and, second, that almost everyone does something well. Third, almost everyone can improve if the system allows or encourages it. Even where there is little incentive for improvement, there is room for diversity in a complex system. Admittedly, hiring criteria and systems of evaluation attempt to reflect diversity, but in practice they too often impose a template on the job and the person. Rather than aid the people and thus the firm in the adaptive process that Darwin described, these practices reward the winners and cull the losers according to the template, not the diverse needs of the firm. The most glaring example of the template is the universal appraisal form for the so-called annual merit reviews—a topic that is discussed in Chapter 5. Other templates are more subtle, but pervasive nevertheless: appearance or behavior that is more narrowly prescribed than generally accepted social norms; knowing when to speak or to be spoken to; strictly adhering to the chain of command and using only accepted channels of communication; "sitting on" important information that might provoke controversy. Certainly, a business, among other things, is a society of people, and some behavior is socially unacceptable. But, in most instances that I have observed, we have emphasized conformity to the detriment of creativity and Darwinian adaptability.

This corrupted Darwinism is beguiling also because it simplifies the tasks of senior executives who under this aegis need only to watch and keep score. They use numbers to measure outcomes, and they delegate to someone else the management of people and processes that produce the outcomes. Convenient and comfortable. Numbers are neat and clean. Human beings are messy and complex. Determining people's areas of competence or their need for coaching and training is a fuzzy, time-consuming task. Allaying their fears and accommodating their wishes are sometimes impossible.

In fairness, senior managers I have known not only express but also manifest their concern with the human side of management. Some are generally well-intentioned, often compassionate, but misdirected nevertheless. Many of them do not understand two critical aspects of a business system: complexity and variation. As Dr. Deming showed us with the flow diagram he introduced in Japan in 1950, and as Dr. Ishikawa elaborated with his celebrated fishbone diagram,[2] the outcomes of any business process are the result of myriad causal elements, all of which are subject to variation. Their combined variation produces variation in the outcome. Then, as Walter Shewhart demonstrated in 1939,[3] if the system is stable, the degree of variation that it produces is predictable with a reasonable degree of belief. Moreover, if the system is stable it can be improved only by improvement of the process, not by tinkering with the most recent data point. However, in business, we often isolate one variable of a stable system and use the most recent data point to analyze the output. This technique does not work unless, by chance, the variable we tinker with accidentally happens to be a key to improving the system. More often, action on the most recent data point of a single component of a system *increases* the variation—just the opposite outcome that we are looking for.

Here is an example from the time-honored monthly financial review. It recalls the accounts receivable example introduced earlier. The isolated variable in this story is Frank, the credit manager. The most recent data point is the month-end number for accounts receivable. Say the AR/DSO (Accounts Receivable/Days Outstanding) have for the last few months been running between 54 and 63 days. Let's also make the simplifying assumption that there is no seasonal variation. Let's say, too, that business has been soft, cash is tight, and that the boss is worried. And this month's AR/DSO has risen to 65 days! The boss may have all the compassion in the world for Frank, the credit manager, but the order goes out: "Frank, bring that receivables number back under 60 days and be quick about it!" Implicit in this is the threat—a poor review, a reduced year-end bonus, or worse.

Alarm bells go off. Frank interrupts the rhythm in his department. Everyone mans the telephones to make collection calls. Frank will make calls on big accounts himself—by pulling in some favors from valued customers, or worse, by alienating some good customers whose accounts are only slightly past due. He might ask permission from the CFO to give anticipation discounts to customers who pay their bills before the due date. If he is both desperate and wily, he will ask his friends in the billing department to delay mailing of invoices for a day or two, a sure-fire method to reduce receivables. Even better, he will convince the accounting department to take a reserve against some of the big, seriously past-due receivables. Now it's a cinch! At the next month's financial review, Frank is the proud owner of a 58-day AR/DSO, one "Attaboy!" and a hint of a promotion. And the boss? He's a born leader. Knows how to get results! "These are good people, but sometimes you just have to put the pressure on." Never mind that there is precious little additional cash, that reported profits are diminished by the reserve against receivables, or that reported sales are diminished by the two-day delay in invoicing! By golly, AR/DSO is in line!

Chances are, however, that AR/DSO will be greater than 65 days sometime during the next few months. Yes, the write-off of past-due receivables will have some long-term effect, but unless the system changes, even they will creep back in over time. Improvement gained by taking reserves against receivables will be offset by the invoices that were held up, now being sent along with the normal month's invoices. Far more serious, however, is the disruption of normal customer communications caused by the marathon telephone collection effort of the credit department. Present customers' phone calls will not have been returned. Recent billing errors will not have been adjusted. Credits for returned merchandise will not have been entered. Normal data entry will have been delayed. It will take months to get back into control.

Forgetting these aberrations, let us touch on the theory that explains why AR/DSO will work back to its normal variation pattern, even why it might deteriorate despite Frank's heroic efforts last month. The process that produced the 65-days AR/DSO was well within the upper and lower control limits of a stable system. This system could have just as easily produced 56 days or 68 days in any given month. One could say in the extreme that Frank is merely flotsam in the stream that produces the AR/DSO outcome. What if customers are not paying because quality is bad? What if billing is late or wrong—freight charges incorrect, proper discounts not given, wrong prices?

What if shipments are delayed en route? What if the wrong item is shipped? What if the product is damaged in shipment, then returned for credit—and the return has not yet been processed? What if salesmen have been overpromising? What if there is a change in the billing cycle or a change in general economic conditions? What if management is reluctant to hurt reported earnings by taking a write-off or reserve against accounts that are probably uncollectible? What does Frank have to do with all of this?

There are two activities in which Frank might influence AR/DSO: credit terms and collection policies. But even these are not in Frank's purview alone. Credit terms are a policy decision. Surprisingly, so is the policy of collection. Ask any credit manager who has clamped down on a big account about the angry phone calls he gets from the sales manager—sometimes from the president of the firm.

All the factors just discussed and many others combine to produce the AR/DSO number. Furthermore, the variation in each of these factors combines to produce a variation in the outcome—AR/DSO. Usually, this variation is random, and its limits are predictable with a reasonable degree of belief. This means that the system that produces 65 days accounts receivable is the same system that produces 58 days. Yet we cheer, we celebrate, we give bonuses for 58 days. We growl, we mope, and we bring out the whips when it is 65 days.

If our threats to Frank do not produce results, we go to the human relations department or we hire a consulting firm to design a new incentive program. The damage from these well-meaning machinations is incalculable. The incentive pay is frittered away; it does not address the causes of excessive AR/DSO; it rewards chance and fortune. Incentive pay pits people in various activities against each other—it pits functions against each other. Variation is amplified, not modulated, as people try to manipulate the outcomes rather than improve the process. Moreover, consider the activities just described in the AR/DSO dance. Did they contribute anything to the real work of the firm—to designing, financing, building, selling, and collecting for a product or service? Precious little! Then consider all the cousins of AR/DSO—all the molehills we turn into mountains, all the misdirected efforts, wasted energy, wasted time.

But the biggest waste of all is the damage to the human spirit, which destroys people's commitments to the aim, mission, and objectives of the firm. People are trying to gain rewards in zero-sum games whose outcomes are dictated by chance and fortune. What senior managers have forgotten is that people doing the work know that in many respects they are merely pawns. They do the best that they can, they play the game, but while playing they wonder who is running the asylum.

Let's now go back to Frank's boss—the born leader—and further explore the two versions of Darwinian economics: the corrupted version—managing the reward system with the numbers; and the productive version—improving the process to meet the challenge to meet a changing, sometimes hostile environment.

The corrupted version often seems reasonable and straightforward. "After all, didn't Frank produce the 58 days AR/DSO when I asked him?" As the foregoing discussion indicated, the number was achieved, but the company was ill-served. The system was not changed; the process was not modified; no enduring, sustainable improvements were made. Instead, the single-minded, almost frantic activities required to make the numbers sowed the seeds of more trouble in the future.

I have studied tens of dozens of so-called incentive plans and have found that although nearly all produce money for the individual participants, none has made a dime for the firm. It is likely that my own experience is limited. Some of my respected colleagues insist that they have been able to measure the incremental contributions to the firm from incentive plans. I only ask them to consider the following questions. Over what period were the returns measured? Did the incentive program expand the market or the market share, or did it just move the sales from one period to another? Were you able to measure all the costs? In the case of a sales manager, did you measure the overtime that might have been required in manufacturing and distribution that was necessary to get the goods out the door? If it was an incentive for manufacturing, did quality stay high and finished goods inventories stay low? If it was an incentive for distribution to lower the unit shipping costs, were full carloads and full truckloads dispatched from the distribution center only to lie around in satellite warehouses or customer back rooms? Were you able to measure the hostility of those in the firm who were not included in the incentive plan? Did you measure the hostility of those who worked heroically to make the target but who missed because of circumstances out of their control?

Even though I have never seen an incentive plan that covered all these costs, such a plan may well exist. Suffice it to say that most of the ones I have studied have not only failed to make money for the firm, they have damaged it.

I am aware that I am blaspheming a time-honored shibboleth, that I am alienating an army of human resource professionals, and that I am kicking a crutch out from under the arms of Frank's boss and his ilk. But I remain steadfast. So-called incentive pay has become a surrogate for leadership, and a poor one at that. Pay for performance, reasonable as it sounds, is almost an oxymoron if the attempt is to tie performance to an individual or a single activity within the firm. Frank cannot, through his actions alone, make a sustainable improvement in the Accounts Receivable/Days Outstanding. Changes are required throughout the various functions of the company. Distribution, order entry, sales, marketing, and the billing department all are involved.

Productive Darwinism

Improvement that will help to ensure the firm's survival and growth can best be achieved when Frank's boss helps to build bridges across the functions. But this cannot be achieved in a climate of suspicion and distrust. If Frank is singled out to receive a reward for actions taken by the group, particularly if the status or pay of others seems to be diminished, the improvement process will self-destruct or sputter to a halt.

The positive aspects of Darwinism—the firm's ability to adapt to a competitive environment—can be achieved under the following conditions: (1) Frank's boss makes certain that data and information are developed about the accounts receivable process, (2) he provides the tools, the techniques, and the time to analyze the problem, (3) he demonstrates his own commitment from time to time by jumping in to help bridge the functions, and (4) he establishes an equitable reward system. Then the positive side of Darwinian economics emerges. The organization may find that the best way to improve AR/DSO is to improve the billing process, to reduce damage in warehousing and shipping, to simplify deals and special offers so the customer's accounts payable department can understand them. AR/DSO is no longer an end in itself. It is a lever to lift the performance of the entire system. If every symptom of a system's malfunction were treated similarly, improvement could be stated in orders of magnitude.

But if we continue to treat the symptoms, not the causes, and if we act as if they were independent of the system, not interdependent, and if we continue to reward individuals when the organization perceives the performance is unfairly evaluated, we will continue to waste precious time and valuable creative potential. My opening premise that half of what's going on in U.S. business is wasted may be conservative.

4

Man Lives by Bread Alone— and Other Flawed Paradigms

Here are three paradigms that have damaged the effectiveness of rewards and recognition in the workplace:

Man lives by bread alone.

There is not enough bread to go around.

He should not enjoy the baking of it.

There is a fourth: "Nor should he enjoy eating it," but that intrudes on the turf of the theological, psychological, and philosophical, so I will excuse it from my deliberations.

The themes of economic man, the zero-sum society, and the Puritan ethic will provide the framework for closer examination of the three paradigms.

Paradigm One: Man Lives by Bread Alone

Rewards would be simple if workers were to leave their human baggage at home: pride, discontent, self-esteem, prejudice, love, envy, yearning, anger, need to belong, need to excel, need to change, fear of change. Not possible! The purely economic man is a myth. And although rationality is a central human characteristic, the simplistic notion of rational man is fiction.[1] Even John Maynard Keynes, with whose conclusions I generally disagree, spoke of the animal spirits of humans. Perhaps he had portents of the neo-Keynesian theorists who would use humans as constants in their Procrustean models.

The concept of the whole human being is not an alien notion. It is the stock in trade of psychologists, psychoanalysts, and psychiatrists. Poets, playwrights, and philosophers have always dealt with the whole man and woman. During the industrial revolution, Robert Browning spoke to businesses directly in the "Song of the Shirt" and "Pippa Passes." Charles Dickens gave us Scrooge and Bob Cratchit to mull over. On the academic front, Maslow developed the idea of self-actualization that was first proposed by Aristotle and developed by John Stuart Mill in the nineteenth century and Kurt Goldstein in the 1930s. Maslow disliked the artificiality of drive theories and wanted to emphasize the unitary characteristic of human motivation. McGregor, who gave us Theory Y, synthesized the work of Drucker and other predecessors. Nevertheless, his formulations broke new ground.[2, 3] After Maslow and McGregor, thousands of others have continued to study and write. Some of their ideas have found their way into the workplace. Other ideas are still tossing about in academic journals. Unfortunately, precious few have been effectively employed.

Our marketing departments have been aware of the whole human being for years, but little has migrated from the advertising we produce to the way we reward and motivate people— even in our marketing departments. Too many of the insights about the whole human being which have warped their way into our business fabric have followed time-worn patterns of company picnics, employee-of-the-month, annual awards banquets, family nights, and the Christmas turkey.

Why haven't we done better? Because it is so difficult! If indeed the economic human is a myth, then monetary rewards alone are insufficient. If humans are not rational, and if they are not similarly irrational, then the design of nonmonetary rewards is monstrously difficult. If it were easy—if humans were merely economic and rational—we could rely on those crusty old war-horses, greed and fear, and let it go at that. As if to prove the exception, a few tyrants have clawed their way to power using greed and fear. They garner a lot of publicity, but they and their enterprises don't last very long. Thoughtful business leaders, however, grapple with more robust rewards that will meet a fuller range of people's needs and concomitantly nurture a business that will thrive in an increasingly complex future. But even these efforts have met with contradiction and failure. Companies have tried Scanlon plans and gain-sharing to better serve economic man. These and similar schemes work for a while—until those periods came along when there were no gains to share. Moreover, the question, "How do you measure gains?" always confounded the issue. Stock options for managers—along with SARs (stock appreciation rights) phantom stock, restricted stock, and various incentive awards based on ROI, ROE, RONA, RONAE, and the rest of the financial alphabet have met similar lack of success.

To serve the whole person we have tried to apply self-actualization ideas that were so well articulated by Maslow, but we have learned that what is actualizing to one is anathema to another. That does not mean that Maslow was wrong. It may mean that we do not yet understand self-actualization. McGregor's elegant Theory Y has, too often, been dished up as permissive mush.

The Golden Rule isn't much help either. Not everyone wants the same things "done unto" them. Not everyone wants to be on a team. Some are stars. Others think they are. Some value security more than pay. Some would trade pay for more time off. Some like piecework. Others wilt under that pressure. Some rise to a challenge. Others prefer support roles. Some have high energy. Others are low key. These differences should confirm that no reward system can meet the specific needs of every individual in the enterprise. It would be foolish of the enterprise to try such a plan and it would be childish of the individual to expect it.

Our approach to rewards sometimes dramatizes the poverty of another tacit assumption—businesses and people are enemies.

Harshly stated, "To keep the people at bay, throw them a bone—even a piece of meat from time to time." This is the extreme, of course, but is a statement that was made to me—not in jest—by the personnel director of a large well-known firm. More advanced reward systems might be compared to the humane treatment of pets. "Make certain they are well-fed and also have a comfortable life—shelter from the elements, medical treatment when needed—and give them a hug or a pat on the head from time to time." Perhaps I am too harsh. Again, the words may be wrong, but the tune is familiar. Reward systems that are even more advanced consider the notion of job enrichment, cross-training, and development of people in order to reduce turnover and to make certain that qualified people are available for job openings. This certainly is on the right track, but the approach is defensive rather than proactive. Until the obvious becomes profound—businesses are people—we will continue to patch together reward schemes that miss the mark. Rather, we should acknowledge that the whole man or woman comes to work. Proper rewards, therefore, are intellectual and emotional as well as economic. For this reason, rewards cannot be separated from the business but *are* business. They are integral to the business activities. Finally, the reward must improve the condition of both—business and people—the system and its components. Such goals are easy to propose but difficult to achieve. Guidelines for their design and implementation will be developed in the next chapter. But first, let's examine more closely the seemingly simple-minded premise—businesses are people.

This certainly is not a revolutionary idea, but its implications need reinforcement. Essentially, all economic input is the result of value that is added by human beings. Iron ore has no economic value until someone digs it out. The equipment that extracts it is assembled by humans. Components of the equipment are made by humans. The raw material that is used to make the components has no value until it is processed by humans. The same holds true for machine tools used in the manufacturing process—and for the facilities. Similarly, distribution costs are human costs. Certainly, administrative, R&D, and selling costs are also. Capital is produced by human efforts. Most land value is a result of human endeavor. Air, sunshine, and water are gifts—unless the air is purified, heated, or cooled, the water is distributed, or the sun's rays are harnessed by solar cells.

The foregoing exemplifies the importance of humans in the production of goods. The human contribution to systems that deliver pure services makes it more apparent that if there is a difference in goods and services, the difference ultimately can be traced to human effort.

Let's be clear. The premise that businesses are people is not a paraphrase of "What's good for General Motors is good for the country," although there is a certain poignancy in that statement today. It does not suggest that people commit a lifetime to the same business enterprise. That smacks of slavery, and the lack of variety may cause loss to both. Nor does it say that businesses should promise lifetime employment. That smacks of paternalism and ignores reality—only the customer can guarantee employment. It does not suggest that business is Big Brother and should take responsibility for people's private lives. It does suggest that businesses—to be worthy of the workers' trust—should demonstrate a genuine concern for people's welfare and general well-being. It suggests that businesses should be humanitarian, go outside the regular rules, and help their people that are in distress.

This is not to say that business should follow them from work to their kitchens and bedrooms. People have lives that are separate from business. But we need to realize that people cannot check business at the door when they arrive home any more than they can check home at the door when they arrive at the workplace. Moreover, they are *whole* human beings in both places. If, while in the workplace, they truly act as the neoclassic version of economic man suggests, they and the business will be poorer for it. It is precisely their "baggage" which was characterized earlier that moves us forward. Their anger, their discontent, their yearnings, their need to excel, their need for change—these transmitted into action can enrich us all. They create the new products and services, new social and economic systems. These are the forces that tranform our lives.

"Aha," I can hear our zealous designers of incentive systems say. "Now, we should design incentives to reward anger, discontent, yearnings, need to excel, and need for change." Ridiculous? Certainly! But no worse in theory than their present practices which break the work and people into piece parts—then try to reward the parts. They are pulling up trees to examine the roots. They are dissecting hearts to find the soul. Did the classical gestaltists live in vain? I thought by now that most everyone acknowledges that the whole is greater than the sum of its parts.

Paradigm Two: There Is Not Enough Bread to Go Around

If a society believes that resources are finite, it will be singularly occupied with their allocation. This preoccupation will confirm the hypothesis. The ensuing struggle for "a fair share" of finite resources will blind the society's members to possibilities for increase. Even if they were to glimpse such opportunities, the allocation struggle would sap the energy required for their pursuit. The more homely example is, "Why waste time fighting over one loaf of bread if we can bake two or ten?"

Most resources are not finite. Moreover, those which are finite are substitutable. If humanity's creative genius is effectively employed, nonrenewable resources which we have used unwisely can be replaced.

If resources are scarce, merely—not finite— improvement, not allocation, must certainly be the incandescent vision. The leader will fail who permits the enterprise to drift into a pattern of squabbling over scarce resources rather than to mobilize energies to increase resources.

Two important caveats, however: Growth for growth's sake is the fountainhead of disaster. Even if growth for growth's sake does not inundate the balance sheet with debt, it suborns judgment as the spate of restructurings, divestitures, and downsizing in the 1980s and 1990s testifies. The second caveat harks back to the flawed paradigm of economic man. Economic growth, while important—crucial in the long term—is only one form of growth. An organization can also grow in terms of its institutional learning. Its members can grow in terms of their skills, knowledge, insight, and judgment. Happily, there are no limits here. These require neither scarce nor finite resources.

Moreover, this noneconomic growth is essential to successful economic growth and requires as much attention from its leaders. Nowhere has it been written on tablets of stone and hurled down from the mountain top that a firm must grow in revenues by 15 percent every year and return an annual 20 percent on equity. There is a season for plowing and a season for harvest. But without proper attention to noneconomic growth, the droughts will be frequent and severe.

Now let's look more specifically at the notion of scarcity. Given the basic nature of man, all resources are scarce. I have never met an executive who would not like to have more resources at her or his command—even though some seem unable to effectively employ the resources they have. Most of us would like to have more money, goods, and services, and for some people there never seems to be enough of anything.

However, most thoughtful people have negotiated a truce among their desires, efforts, and abilities. This does not mean that these people will not answer the call to improve the output of the system. They will be delighted to participate in the endeavor if they believe that the distribution of rewards is fair. Moreover, they usually understand—or are open to understanding—what "fair" really means. I have found, consistently, that most people understand the financial requirements of a business system—that debt and equity must be served, that capital for growth is required. They will not understand, nor will they willingly answer the call, if rewards to any one part of the system seem excessive. The leader's most important tasks are to prevent the excesses, to successfully communicate a sense of parity, then to nurture the motivation, tools, knowledge, and skills necessary for the improvement of the system and all its members. A leader's most profound failure is to foster or to permit the wasted efforts and energy found in adversarial systems fostered by notions of excesses and zero sum.

In earlier chapters, we have visited many of the artifacts of zero-sum assumptions that foster adversarial behavior. Here are others—from organized labor, government, and media—that are taking their toll on our ability to compete.

Let's look first at the dubious contributions of collective bargaining—certainly an adversarial activity: different pay for different work, work rules which govern who gets paid for what, seniority systems, shift differentials, coffee breaks, mandatory times for setups, and other limits on productivity. These have, in successive bargaining sessions, ratcheted some companies into near immobility. Other fruit from this vineyard has been more pay for less work. In addition to vacations which generally are richly deserved, we have guaranteed sick days, and that mockery of common sense—bonuses to people for not taking sick days. We have personal days and birthdays. The trade union lobby and lawmakers have given us paternity days, election days, ethnic days, and a host of other special observances. We have Christmas and Christmas Eve, Good Friday and Easter, in addition to other religious days. We have New Year's Day, President's Day, Martin Luther King Day, Memorial Day, the Fourth of July, Labor Day, and Thanksgiving. Moreover, the highways are full in the early afternoons preceding and the mornings following these days. In addition, some of the ideas behind work rules and shop floor practices have migrated to the entire work force. Work rules have turned into precise, rigid job descriptions. "Write-ups for screw-ups" have turned into written performance reviews. Time clocks, those paradigms of mistrust, have found their way into nonunionized offices and retail establishments. Some of these anachronisms have become laws of the land, results of the holy crusade against business by trade unions and government, usually aided by hostile media. Many of their attacks are richly deserved. We in business are sometimes our own worst enemies. We deserve the intent, if not the administration, of some of our restrictive laws. But some of the attacks from news actors and artists, writers, and producers in television and motion pictures are savagely unfair. Their purposes sometime seem to be to politicize, not to illumine, improve, or even to entertain.

A few labor leaders are beginning to understand that labor is part of a larger system. They are beginning to act as if their goals are more nearly congruent with those of society. But the adversarial climate still prevails—on both sides of the table. I further acknowledge that a few elected government officials are seen as pro-business. However, anti-business bias is deeply ingrained in legislative staffs and in the bureaucracy that administers their laws. If history follows its course, meaningful change will not occur until provoked by a cataclysm. Pray that we have the wisdom to rewrite history.

The constraints just described clearly are born of adversarial proceedings. Implicit in these proceedings is the flawed concept of limited resources. The supply of food, clothing, and other goods and services—the rewards for our activities—are finite, and we must fight for our share. We cannot trust each other to see that they are distributed equitably. We do not even trust that a society governed by laws would provide for their equitable distribution. So we have designed a society of constraints. Think of the improvement, however, if we could begin to truly understand that each of us is part of a system. When one of us is hurt, we are all hurt. Yet some pernicious madness pushes us to continue hurting each other—crippling the system in which we live. Back to the theory of holes. We just keep digging. If all of us—business, trade unions, and government—do not act swiftly to remove excessive constraints on output, "there's not enough to go around" will indeed be the correct paradigm.

Paradigm Three: He Should Not Enjoy the Baking of It

Recently, a director of research told me he was leaving his prestigious job because it was not fun anymore. Later I found that he had taken a less important job at less pay at a location that required him to move from an area that he and his family loved. Such is the power of joy in work.

"Are you having fun?" Dr. Deming recalls Willis Whitney's greetings to his colleagues when he was director of the General Electric Laboratories. Joy in work rewards both the individual and the enterprise. Years ago, as a lay minister, I delivered a sermon entitled "Creation and the Ode to Joy," drawing on Schiller's great poem and using the music from the fourth movement of Beethoven's *Ninth Symphony*. The central theme of the sermon was that true joy came from creating something of value. People who enjoy what they're doing are more productive. Productive people usually enjoy their work. The job of the leader is to enhance the opportunity for joy. At the least, celebrate small victories, be liberal with praise when it is warranted, build on strength rather than dwell on weakness! Or, if the going is tough with no end in sight, pave the way for progress by providing some relief. Someone once said, "The job of the teacher is not to remove pain—but to help the student bear the pain." No job will be consistently satisfying. Some jobs will be long, tough, sometimes grinding. But just as the wise captain knows when shore leave is more important than more training, the wise leader knows when to say, "Let's quit early and go have a beer."

Think of your own experience when the light bulb turned on, illuminating some long-sought-for insight or solution. Many of those happy occasions, I wager, came not during teeth-gritting and head-banging, but unexpectedly. Certainly, intensive skull-work or downright drudgery is required; but the breakthroughs often come when the pressure is off.

All who study human nature and understand something about the human performance know the relationships among productivity, therapeutic diversion, joy, and pride of workmanship or accomplishment. But perhaps the most useful construct would be to hark back to our earlier theme: Businesses are people. Most of us spend our lives at work or thinking about work. What a shame if there were no joy in it.

5

Comprehensive Compensation— a New Concept

I witnessed a near-debacle recently when an experienced human relations professional introduced a new executive pay plan at the firm's annual management meeting. He was pelted by the corporate version of brickbats, dead cats, and rotten tomatoes as he tried to defend his new scheme. About two-thirds of the audience insisted that the plan was unfair. The one-third that seemed to support the general thrust of the plan sided with the others in the conclusion that the plan was too complicated—much too hard to understand. Similar scenes are being played throughout the corporate world, and they relate to all levels of the hierarchy, not just the executives.

How to compensate people is one of the toughest questions that managers must answer. Countless hours are spent not only by personnel specialists, but by people in every function and at every level, including the boardroom. Compensation issues are so thorny that work stoppages occur in their name. Even more costly than work stoppages is a sullen, dispirited work force that believes that compensation is inadequate or unfairly distributed. Productivity is lost as people divert their attention from the firm's work to their own issues, ranging from damaged egos to keeping food on the table.

Because compensation issues run the gamut of human complexity, they will always be thorny. But they need not be as difficult as we have made them. In efforts to fine-tune compensation, we often overcomplicate it. The fine-tuning, instead of reducing points of contention, often multiplies them. Moreover, the underlying theory of many compensation packages seems to support the flawed premises that were introduced in preceding chapters: Businesses and people are enemies, and people are merely economic rational beings whose human needs should be checked at the entry doors of the workplace.

Criticism carries the responsibility for remedy. Accordingly, I will suggest a concept of compensation that will reduce complexity and eliminate many of the pressure points that prompt adversarial behavior. In addition, this concept will reflect the symbiosis that exists between the firm and the individual. Furthermore, the concept I propose will consider the needs of the whole human being, not just the hollow human who is contemplated by the antiquated notion of economic man. Finally, this new concept of compensation will address the five causes of mistrust: the misalignment of measurement and rewards, incompetence or the presumption of incompetence, lack of appreciation for a system, unreliable information, and integrity failure.

The suspicious reader may now be alarmed. "Where is this leading?" "Are we being asked to forget about the watchwords of the nineties—accountability and pay for performance or those stalwarts of the seventies and eighties, management by objectives,[1] share of market, ROI, ROE, RONAE, and the other financial measures?" "Does increased emphasis on the system produce results or just a warm, fuzzy feeling?" "Doesn't employee involvement lead to anarchy?" "What is the role of the leader and manager in this new scheme?" "What happens to the bottom line?" To meet the concern of the suspicious reader, I promise to address these traditional concepts. However, I will suggest different methods of dealing with them from those that are currently employed. But I impose three important caveats. First, one should be careful about changing the reward system unless one is prepared also to change management methods, policies, and procedures. If, for instance, you are using numerical targets as surrogates for managing—rather than helping employees to bridge the functions so that they can attack causes rather than symptoms—then this new reward system might lead to loss of control. Second, employees and employers alike should be advised that the new compensation method I propose is much more demanding than those currently in use. Employees will be expected to produce more and better results, to consistently improve their performance, to pitch in and help others when appropriate. No more hiding behind wooden job descriptions, just making quota, or watching the clock. There will be no room for slackers and malcontents.

Managers' jobs will also be more demanding. Instead of setting quotas and numerical targets, then rewarding those who make the numbers and penalizing those who do not, managers in this brave new world will be expected to produce financial results and at the same time to have intimate knowledge of the components of the system they are managing, then be creative enough and effective enough to improve it constantly. Moreover, managers will be expected to develop people who can continue to meet greater challenges. The third caveat is also important—no compensation plan that I know of is fully transportable from one organization to another. No plan can prescribe an always-appropriate mix of employee benefits, perks, deferred compensation, stock options, or similar benefits. It is impossible to create a template to which other companies should conform. Although I have, as a turnaround manager, employed all the elements of the theory that I propose, my method of application is necessarily different from those of the many other firms that are now adopting the general concepts that I propose. Although the specifics will differ, the underlying theory is discussed almost daily in the business press. It is a concept whose time has come. Here are its elements.

1. Treat people with respect.
    a. Trust their judgment. Share necessary information.
    b. Have great expectations.
    c. Hold people accountable for the following:

       (1) Activities for which they have nominal control

       (2) Activities in their spheres of influence which they do not control

       (3) Proficiency in their specialty or area of activity

       (4) Continued improvement in their specialty

       (5) Readiness to take on new assignments

       (6) Working cooperatively with their colleagues

       (7) Keeping the customer in view

       (8) Performing their jobs in a manner that will build trust

    d. Provide people with the tools, training, and information to do the job.

    e. Provide regular, honest, actionable feedback.

2. Pay at market or better.

    a. Let market forces determine basic pay ranges for each job, then beat that when possible.

    b. Avoid the cost and adversarial activity caused by the administration of differential merit increases or individual incentive pay.

3. Promote thoughtfully and carefully.

    a. Make decisions based on long-term evaluation.

    b. Use informal feedback from the candidates' peers, subordinates, internal and external customers—as well as superiors.

4. Hire carefully and thoughtfully.

    a. Base decisions not only on skills but on ability and commitment to learning and growth.

    b. Base decisions on the candidate's perceived ability to work productively in your environment.

5. Produce a quality product or service.

    a. Pride in work and accomplishment is powerful compensation.

    b. Pride in the enterprise is also rewarding.

6. Remove from the organization anyone who overtly violates trust.

7. If people, making good faith efforts, do not perform satisfactorily, find out why. Reassign or retrain them. If unsuccessful, remove them from the organization—with dignity and respect.

8. When times are tough, share the pain.

9. When times are good, share the gain.
10. Provide leadership that will build trust.

Let's look closer at these things. Some will be straightforward. Others, like the controversial concepts of accountability and control, will require detailed discussion.

1. Treat people with respect.

a. Trust their judgment.

Share as much information as possible about the aim, mission, and values of the firm. Provide a rich understanding of how employees' specific missions and supporting objectives relate to the aims and values of the firm. People who know "why" can add more value than those who merely know "how." Then, solicit their ideas. Actively listen to and act on their ideas about improvements of the product or service. Both the employee and the business will be richer for the effort. Do not fall into the trap of paying for specific ideas or unusual effort. Under the compensation guidelines proposed here, the employees are rewarded when the enterprise is rewarded, not only with money but with greater prospects for security if that is what they desire, and with the satisfaction of a job well done.

b. Have great expectations.

Expecting people to perform poorly, then making up for their shortcomings with excessive supervision and control is a form of economic slavery that neither the firm nor the individual should tolerate. Costs soar. Self-esteem plummets. Soldiering, working by the book, slowdowns, and other manifestations of adversarial intent compensate no one. Conversely, when people understand and willingly accept the aim, vision, and values of the firm, when they are provided with the tools and training to do the job, and when they believe they are treated fairly, they will usually exceed targets set by industrial engineers or unimaginative bosses. Moreover, these employees will be rewarded by pride in their accomplishment and joy in their work.

c. Hold people accountable.

Just as low expectations communicate disrespect, so does excuse from accountability. Knowing that people depend on you, then delivering on that promise, is enormously rewarding to the healthy human psyche. But accountability is a complex issue. On the one hand, people should always stretch their imaginations, use their negotiating skills, and be ready to put forth heroic efforts to achieve goals that at the outset may seem unachievable. Nearly all people have the potential to transcend their apparent abilities, and in the process of doing so enrich themselves as well as the enterprise. On the other hand, when people use heroic efforts to meet narrowly focused goals, and when they do it in a manner that is detrimental to other parts of the organization, accountability can backfire. In this respect, people should always know the aim, vision, mission, value, goals, and objectives of the firm. Employees should have an appreciation for other functions and activities. Then people not only can avoid damaging other components of the system, they can work to improve the system.

But the evaluation of an individual's efforts must be made by a leader who knows something about variation. Whereas performances of individuals differ, they usually differ within a range that indicates that improvement of the system in which the individual works is more important than singling out an individual for improvement and leaving the system alone. Moreover, the leader who understands variation will also understand the importance of observing people's performance over time—with consideration not of quantitative output alone but also of the differences and difficulties of the tasks that they perform.

The vagaries of the measurement methods and tools as well as normal variation in performance make it both difficult and dangerous to evaluate individual performance independently of a system. This does not deny that people are different. Over time, differences can be observed and generalizations can be made. Some people will consistently perform better than their peers, some will be better suited to the work, some will pick up the slack when others get behind, some will add value through their creative contributions. Some indeed will be true outliers of the performance distribution. But evaluation of their performance should consider all these factors—and more.

The evaluation is not only, "Did he meet the goal?" but "Did he meet it responsibly?" or "If she did not meet the goal that was given at the outset, was she able to modify it, improve on it, or redirect it in order to acknowledge different realities? Were the people who helped her along the way left exhausted and bitter, or were they just plain tired but exhilarated, ready for new and greater challenges?" Numbers alone cannot tell the story. The company that is governed by "Just give me the bottom line...I don't care how you do it" will generally destroy itself. And finally, one of the worst things about narrowly focused numerical goals in the "bottom line" environment is that goals are often too low. They can limit the imagination. Worse, managers who could exceed their goals will only meet them for fear that their superior performance will be the floor from which next year's goals will be racheted.

As the foregoing has suggested, accountability predictably evokes debate about control. The argument is that one cannot be held accountable for those activities which one does not control. As usual, polarization flaws the debate. We juxtapose independence and interdependence, control and predestination. On the softer side is the notion that humans have almost no control over their activities—that their actions are preordained, or so intertwined with the system in which they operate that they are virtually powerless. Alternatively, the human either stands as the Rock of Gibraltar, immovable, or overcomes almost insurmountable obstacles with prodigious feats. The answer, of course, is at neither pole. Its location is defined by parties of good faith who are working toward a common goal. The dichotomies are not only irrelevant, they are misleading and harmful. They are based on the following misconceptions:

- We can plan with precision.
- We can describe with precision.
- We can execute with precision.

These are joined by the following misperceptions:

- The system remains the same when one of its components is changed.

- The system has no ability to correct itself.
- The system itself is not accountable.

Finally, we have the following misbelief:

- The individual is necessarily suffocated by the system.

Let's look at these in turn.

We can plan with precision.   Holding someone accountable requires that we decide what he is accountable for. This in turn requires planning. Planning in turn requires prediction. Although prediction is requisite for knowledge,[2] predictions are necessarily wrong. If they were right, life would be much easier. If they were precisely right, humankind would be vastly different. It follows, then, that accountability is provisional. The outcomes should be expressed in ranges—plus or minus some amount, approximately this or that. And the method of reaching the outcome cannot be explicitly described—which leads to the second misconception.

We can describe with precision.   For purposes of this discussion, let's examine the use of the annual budget. Holding people accountable for their various pieces of the annual budget implies that not only can we plan with precision, but we can precisely describe the specific tasks or outcomes. Why are departmental or functional budgets necessarily imprecise? Because a change in one activity usually causes change in another! A 10 percent increase in unit sales is generally impossible without a corresponding increase in manufacturing and distribution activity. As these changes are transmitted through the system, they have varying impacts on the outcomes of individual cost components. Some of these components are sensitive to volume, others are sensitive to timing or investment. So our budget, which indeed is useful for planning, is imprecise when used by itself as the only measure of accountability.

We can execute with precision.   Sometimes we can, sometimes we cannot. Much depends on the nature of the task. Assemblers of electronic circuitry, watchmakers, and diamond cutters work with near-precision. The tasks are clearly circumscribed and the training to perform the task is focused and intense.[3] It is foolish to extend to the sales or plant manager, or the director of marketing and finance, those same expectations of near-precision. Their jobs are more complex, in part because of their interdependence with external activities that are integral to their own performance. Indeed, the difficulties associated with planning and describing suggest that executing with precision might not be as important as using our unique humanness to adjust, adapt, and improve. The millennium has not arrived. We should continue to expect more of humans than we do of robots.

The foregoing leads to the three misperceptions about systems which were listed earlier.

The system remains the same when one of its components is changed. Of course it does not! Everything must adapt to some degree. The customer's request to delay a shipment affects distribution, sometimes backs up to manufacturing, which in turn affects purchasing. The delay in booking an account receivable may or may not offset the payable for raw materials or components. Thousands of these adjustments must be made daily, even in a medium-size business.

The system has no ability to correct itself. The response to this misperception is not an argument for anthropomorphism; humans within the system working in concert can make the adjustments that will appear seamless to the outside world. The implicit assumption, of course, is that everyone in the system is pulling in the same direction, working for a common goal. I have witnessed this delightful phenomenon on several occasions, once in a near-crisis situation when a team of professionals pitched in to get a shipment out to a big customer who was about to defect. No job descriptions were necessary, no memos were written, no reports filed. And if one member of the group was not sure what to do, others took up the slack. Both trust and respect were hallmarks of the effort. How do you determine, let alone measure, accountability in this situation? Furthermore, doesn't this process seem to have attractiveness even to a workplace which is not in crisis?

The system itself is not accountable. I hope the foregoing discussions have laid this misperception to rest. In the hierarchy of accountability, certainly more control is held by the system than by any of its components, animate or inanimate. Even the system is subject to external factors which it does not control. But that does not excuse it or the components from applying the resources at their command that reasonably can be brought to bear on achieving the desired outcome.

The individual is necessarily suffocated by the system. The idea of accountability has set up a false dichotomy between the individual and the group—or system. On the one hand, John Wayne, one of my heroes in person and in his roles, conquered almost insurmountable odds with his grit and courage. But the West is won, and John Wayne is gone. On those occasions when John Wayne's individualism is called for, it should be applied. But increasingly, individuals are limited in the amount they can do without help from others. Even John Wayne knew how and when to extract that support.

Support for the thesis that the individual is not necessarily submerged by the group comes also from discussions with executives, who often volunteer that some of their most memorable and rewarding experiences have come from group activities: team sports, playing in a band or orchestra, singing in a church choir, brainstorming and other group problem solving, meeting a deadline, serving on a design team—yes, even military service, especially combat. Contribution to a group effort does not debase the individual. In fact, the way we sometimes play out the rite of individualism backfires when we celebrate one person to the detriment of another. In these instances, individualism runs the risk of being corrupted as individuals who gain power climb up the ladder. Sometimes a misdirected sense of responsibility and accountability pushes them into command and control modes, which may be necessary for short periods during crises—but if command and control methods turn followers into automatons, the leader becomes increasingly lonely and ineffective. Moreover, the leader's style might have so narrowly defined accountability that subordinates, in sullen resignation, give what is asked for—nothing more, sometimes less.

Accountability, then, is a very difficult subject, made more difficult when tied to the distribution of rewards. Even so, accountability is observable, perhaps even measurable—over time. The criteria listed at the beginning of this section will suffice to determine whether one has acted accountably.[4] Let's look at them in turn.

c. Hold people accountable.

(1) *For activities over which they have nominal control.* Repeated failures might suggest that the system is flawed. If this is not the case, repeated failures might suggest deficiencies in people's motivation or ability and will probably require that they be retrained, given different or less demanding tasks, or removed from the organization. This is necessary because the damage to the output usually exceeds the loss from the underperforming unit if the organization repeatedly is required to make up the shortfall of one of its components.

(2) *For activities in their spheres of influence which they do not control.* Solomon himself could not adequately describe all the tasks necessary for the operation of a complex activity. Rigid, narrowly applied job descriptions have failed. Witness what happens in a "job action" when employees decide to "work by the book." The system falls apart. Productivity plummets. Instead, the intent to perform with excellence must be there. Such intent also includes picking up the ball if someone else drops it—or helping an associate who is temporarily overwhelmed or gets behind in her or his work. That intent, however, is empty unless the people know the aim, vision, and values of the enterprise, as well as the specific nature of their mission and objectives which support the attainment of that mission. And the intent is subverted when rewards are tied to zero-sum or to narrowly focused activities rather than to the vitality of the enterprise.

(3) *For proficiency in their specialty or area of activity.* The presumption is that people are provided with the information, tools, and training requisite for the job. If after repeated attempts they cannot perform the task, they should be retrained, reassigned, or removed.

(4) *For continued improvement in their specialty.* People should be encouraged and expected to suggest new ways of doing their jobs, even ways of eliminating their jobs if the task can be eliminated through redefinition or reengineering. (The underlying assumption here is that another job will be available.)

(5) *For readiness to take on new assignments.* If tasks do not change, the product or service will not change. Hiding behind narrowly defined job descriptions and protecting the turf that surrounds the job enervate the organization.

(6) *For working cooperatively with their colleagues.* Self-aggrandizement to the detriment of the organization's goals cannot be tolerated. Again, the presumption is that the reward system fosters cooperation.

(7) *For keeping the customer in view.* Not just internal customers, but external customers, whether they are resellers or end users. No matter how circumscribed the task, the worker should relate it to the ultimate goal—getting and keeping profitable customers. Of course, the company has responsibility also to provide the information that connects the task to the customer and to provide as much opportunity as practical for direct contact with the customer. (More than half of Baldridge Award–recipient Zytec's employees had direct customer contact in 1991.)

(8) *For performing their jobs in a manner that will build trust.* Again, a shared responsibility of the organization and the individual. But especially if the organization has removed the impediments to trust which are described in this book, then individuals should be held accountable for fostering trust. If they see progress only as zero-sum, and act as though their progress can come only at the expense of others, they should be counseled. If counseling fails, they should be removed.

These eight aspects of accountability can only rarely be measured with numbers. Nor can they be properly derived from the blanks we fill out or the attributes we check off on the time-honored form which we use for merit reviews. How well a person discharges his or her accountability can be determined only by a hands-on management that knows enough about the person's job, that observes first-hand, talks to peers, subordinates and customers—external and internal.

d. Provide the tools, training, education, and information to do the job.

Tools alone will not suffice. There are plenty of horror stories about capital expenditures that actually diminish productivity— about computer-based information or decision support systems that have institutionalized bad practice or created unnecessary complexity. But the proper tools in the hands of competent workers who know their jobs are a powerful combination.

Training is addressed in Chapter 10. Suffice it to say that, particularly in today's knowledge-based environment, constant training, including cross-training, is required for success. More than training, provide the opportunity for continuous education. Competition does not stand still. The education received 20 years ago may no longer be adequate. Compensation is negative if employees or executives know they are not competent. This unhappy condition heightens uncertainty and creates a debilitating fear.

Many businesses seem paranoid when it comes to sharing information. Either that or they believe that employees and managers are not competent to understand the information that is available—which, of course, is a self-fulfilling prophecy. In some instances, the competitor's intelligence system has gathered more information about a company's costs, products, and customers than is available to the company's own employees. Certainly, some information should be classified, but much that is classified should not be.

e. Provide regular, honest, and actionable feedback.

The three most important reasons for feedback are (1) to improve the enterprise, (2) to improve the contribution of the person to whom the feedback is given, and (3) to improve the performance of the system and its leaders. Most reviews are judgmental only—used for ranking people or for determining merit pay or individual incentive bonuses. Even if those evaluations are on the mark—or even close—their unintended effects are disastrous.

It was stated earlier and will be developed later that different people and different jobs deserve different pay, but the traditional merit review is a poor tool for making that determination. Companies especially should avoid the disrespect communicated by annual merit reviews which use explicit or implicit numerical indicators—1 through 5, or "outstanding" to "poor." Even though numbers might indicate the feelings of the person doing the rating, they block meaningful interchange. The employee hears nothing until the number is assigned and hears nothing after it is spoken. Numerical indicators are even more destructive if a forced distribution or numerical ranking is implied. Complex tasks performed by complex humans cannot be described by digits. Moreover, a forced distribution could skew unqualified people toward the top or those who are qualified toward the bottom of the ranking. Furthermore, rankings of people are meaningless if jobs are different. Do we penalize the waiter because he cannot cook, the cook because he cannot tie a cash projection to a balance sheet? Even if job and human complexities could be captured by numbers, the implicit distribution of winners and losers fosters adversarial behavior. Another problem with the annual merit review is revealed by its name. Do we really aim to give feedback only once a year? Semiannual reviews are better—quarterly, even better—but why tie them to the calendar? The wise, involved supervisor knows when to leave people alone to work things out for themselves and when to give them feedback.

Here are three suggestions:

- The CEO of a large, diversified firm reviews each of his direct reports at least four times a year in the following way: He writes on one sheet of paper three things that he believes the executive has done well. On another sheet he writes three aspects of the executive's performance that he thinks could be improved. Then, he and his associate use these two pieces of paper as a basis for at least a one-hour open, frank discussion.

- It should not be necessary to offer the second suggestion— but the review process is so threatening that reviewers tend to equivocate. Honesty, forthrightness, sometimes bluntness, are hallmarks of a good review. Painful as it may be, people need to know where they stand. Moreover, if the reviewer's facts or perceptions are wrong, the person being reviewed needs the opportunity for rebuttal. It is not fair to the employee or the firm if the reviewer harbors a misconception. A caution about honesty and bluntness! Stick with specifics. Avoid generalizations. One of the indicators of a healthy psyche is the ability to differentiate between "I did a bad thing" and "I am a bad person." There is a world of difference between "John, you sure screwed up that last customer shipment" and "John, you just aren't cut out for line management, and you can't handle that kind of responsibility. You should be in a staff position." When I graduated from college I went to a placement firm, which administered a battery of tests. The woman who evaluated the tests took me into a small counseling room, closed the door, and intoned, "You are hamperingly self-conscious. You should never be in sales." Perhaps I am hamperingly self-conscious, although I don't know what that means, and I have been selling ever since. All amateur psychologists and most professionals are dangerous—when they try to confine a complex human being into one of their arcane pigeonholes.

- The third suggestion is one that I have used with varying degrees of success. I have asked those who report directly to me to review my performance. After a general discussion, I ask specifically whether I have done things that either they thought were unfair or that hindered them in the discharge of their own responsibilities. Variability in the success of this task comes from initial reluctance to open up from those being reviewed, particularly if they have been accustomed to a closely-managed, authoritarian environment. Time is required to build the trust that will allow them to be direct and honest in their appraisal.

The topics of employee reviews cannot be left without a nod to the legal issues—a nod, not a deep bow. Far too many of the crimes committed in the annual merit review process seek vindication by legal requirements. Affirmative action, gray power, glass ceilings, and symptoms of other deep ills are not exculpated by the tedious annual review forms and numerical ratings. Indeed, numerical ratings can backfire. The legal defense against a suit from a terminated employee whose ratings averaged 4.3 when those of a survivor averaged 3.9 could be made difficult—regardless of the job requirements, which could not be expressed in numbers.

Performance reviews are important management tools. They provide a basis for improving the enterprise, they provide necessary history, particularly in large organizations, and when properly handled they are fair to the employee and the firm. But as in the issues of accountability and control, they are unfair if they are too narrowly defined and if they are numerically expressed.

2. Pay at market or better.

Far too much is made of average hourly pay or annual salaries. What you get is often much more important than what you pay. I would gladly pay a 15 percent premium over the prevailing rate to avoid onerous union work rules. In other instances, isn't it worth a premium in pay to have a team of world-class professionals who are able to perform a wide range of tasks in addition to their specialties and who are committed to the aims of the firm—who are motivated to do their best?

Paying according to market or better also acknowledges the reality of a monetary meritocracy. Some people will be paid more than others. (I am aware of market imperfections. For instance, I doubt that other organizations would hire at the same rate of pay those executives who in 1991 were paid $70 or $80 million. But I know of several boards of directors that would crawl through broken beer bottles to get Jack Welch of GE for $10 or $15 million.) Regardless of present imperfections, however, the market is generally a proper analogue. If the market rate is $200,000 a year for a vice president of marketing for firms of your size in your industry, you would be foolish to offer $100,000 regardless of the intrinsic rewards you might offer, even though there is plenty of evidence that people will take some reduction in pay to avoid onerous working conditions or to have the opportunity to grow.

Paying at market or better does not necessarily mean rigid adherence to salary surveys or close observance of job descriptions and corresponding pay bands. We depend too much on bureaucratic mechanisms in salary negotiations. Perhaps we do so to avoid the stress of looking another human being in the face and explaining in a straightforward manner what we think the job is worth, and in our estimation, how much the employee or manager should be paid. Better to turn the problem over to the personnel officer who can tell the employee which slot he or she fits. Moreover, many business leaders and middle managers dread the prospect of negotiating with prospective employees who feel that they are worth more than the proposed amount. In part, the reluctance of these managers to negotiate is prompted by concern that if they acquiesce to higher pay to one, they will create jealousy among other employees who, precautions to the contrary notwithstanding, nearly always find out how much their co-workers are paid. Tiny Tim is purported to have said, "You become what you eat." Accordingly, I believe that we in business have exacerbated the pecking order problem with our preoccupation with job descriptions, narrow pay bands, and a mechanistic approach to compensation. I am not suggesting that we throw the notion of market parity to the winds, but I am suggesting that, too often, we allow the employment decision to be made on the basis of pay alone, to the detriment of the very important aspects of compensation. Either we fail to communicate properly, or we might be dealing with someone who is concerned only with dollars, in which case both we and the prospective employee will be better off if he or she seeks employment elsewhere.

Paying at market or better can be accomplished in several ways. One is to set base pay at market or better, grant salary raises as the market dictates, and pay no bonuses. This provides apparent stability for the employee and predictability for the company's personnel costs. Large firms in seemingly stable industries who have a risk-averse work force may prefer this to a scheme where part of the pay is pegged to company performance. However, employees should think carefully, particularly in today's roller-coaster environment, about any cherished notion of stability. For some, it might not be a question of having part of their pay at risk. If times get tough enough, all their pay might be at risk.

Another method is to pay salaries at or below market and to pay substantial bonuses (to everyone—more about this later) according to the firm's performance. This puts part of the pay at risk, but, if conditions warrant, it provides the opportunity for pay well above market. The point has been made repeatedly that a business is a system of human beings and other components working toward a common aim. Employees and managers are part of that system. In order to preserve the system, they should be willing to share both the gain and the pain. This is not said with puritanical intent, nor is it suggested as an "incentive" to make people work harder. It is merely to provide the system with flexibility—particularly important in these uncertain times.

However, if too much is at risk, people are so apt to be preoccupied with pay that their performance will suffer. They have plans to make and children to send to college. But I believe that the fortunes of the company and its people are so intertwined that a part of compensation should be tied to company performance.[5]

For instance, an entrepreneurial "start-up" may want to set base pay under the market and then establish a bonus potential of 40 percent of base pay, which would pay 20 percent if the company performed well and up to 40 percent if it performed superbly. More stable companies may wish to use 20 or 30 percent as target bonuses. If performance were unsatisfactory there would be no bonus. Furthermore, the assessment of whether the firm's performance is good, superb, or lousy cannot be tied to the bottom line alone. All financial indicators are arbitrary to some extent. Those that seem most arbitrary are those whose numerators and denominators both are subject to change by short-term decisions. For that reason, companies should think carefully before using those time-honored targets, return on investment, return on equity, or return on capital employed. High investment, which may be exactly right for long-term performance, pumps up the denominator, and the numerator is diminished by high depreciation. Short-term profits are hurt. Other sources of extreme variability are driven by tax and capitalization decisions. High debt can severely diminish after-tax earnings, even though it might pump up earnings per share. Gross margin is often the best financial indicator of long-term operational health, even though it is affected to some extent by depreciation. Whatever indicators are used, they should never be used as guarantees. If profits are hurt by investment decisions, it could mean that they previously had been boosted by lack of investment, which in turn could have been detrimental to the firm. Perhaps cash is hurt, even though reported profits are good. If bonuses are in cash, and the company believes it unwise to borrow to pay them, bonuses may need to be pared back.

There is an obvious drawback to using financial indicators as guidelines rather than guarantees. The seeming uncertainty could create a "We don't trust you" problem—which of course indicates a problem more serious than the bonus decision alone. Bonus pay plans, along with other management practices that are described in this book, require a high degree of two-way communication. Decisions that affect performance—for good or for ill—should be fully communicated to everyone involved as early as possible. If it appears in September that bonuses might be lower than last year's, or pared back altogether, the reasons should be fully communicated and should be disseminated in plenty of time for people to adjust their financial plans. Doubting Thomases who would suggest that such a communiqué would cause people to coast for the rest of the year are either guided by the carrot-and-stick fallacy or believe that managers are helpless to manage.

How does one deal with differential merit increases in this system of compensation? To quote Dr. Deming's succinct response, "Abolish them." Shocking? Perhaps! Un-American? Not at all! Cleansing? Absolutely! Rarely has so much well-meaning effort been so naively spent in order to promote anger, jealousy, and dissention. "Whoa," you say! "How do we reward excellence? How do we motivate people?" Let's deal with the second question first. Perhaps a few will be motivated to "do better" if they received only a 3.9 percent pay increase, when they knew that the pool available for raises was 4.3 percent. Most, however, are turned off. Moreover, trying to determine who gets 4.6 percent, who gets 4.3 percent, or 3.6 percent implies precision that just does not exist—but it does create jealousy among all those who receive less than 4.6 percent.

In a discussion during June 1992 with 24 senior executives of a leading global company, I learned that unanimously they believed that differential merit pay was wasted. It did not motivate them, and they did not believe that it motivated their subordinates. In the same month, 20 executives of a company that had just completed a difficult year unanimously agreed that the company wasted the 3.9 percent pool that was provided for raises. "They should have reinvested the money to provide more security for the future." After reasonable needs have been met, short-term pay is not an effective motivator. I am aware that there are those who disagree, and I respect their sincerity—but increasingly, I have found that merit pay creates more pain than gain.

The question naturally follows, "How, then, do we reward excellence?" First, we cannot properly reward excellence with money alone. Second, we need to define excellence. The difficulty of these two requirements suggests that the comprehensive plan that I am proposing not only expects excellence but pays for it at marketplace rates which reflect excellence. It compensates the whole human being and the system as well. Another answer to rewarding excellence is, "Through promotion." But that answer is incomplete. First, if we are successful in reducing pay bands and layers in the organization, there will be fewer promotions. The Zytec Corporation rewards its hourly employees with incremental raises for successful completion of cross-training. Its executives report that after a few false starts, the system is working satisfactorily. My hunch is that it is satisfactory, in part, because there is a stipulated agreement on the definition of excellence: cross-training.

Defining excellence more precisely might be a full employment act for human resource professionals but is about as precise as counting the number of angels that can dance on the head of a pin. Let's confound the issue of defining excellence by adding the time dimension and the variability introduced by those who make the evaluation. By focusing on the most recent data point—the preceding quarter or year—we lose sight of the past, and we may lose sight of the potential contribution from the person who is being evaluated. In any event, using the last data point focuses the firm and its employees on the short term. Sometimes, the short term is the correct focus, but the consequences are well known when short-term decisions overpower long-term considerations.

Now, let's look at the variability introduced by the customary process of allocating merit pay. First, some executives, like teachers, are tougher graders than others. Where is parity here? Second, the relationship is different between each boss and employee. The same person might receive significantly different reviews from different reviewers. Not only does this variability fail to motivate, it confuses; and it amplifies variation, as hundreds of employees try to "psyche out" dozens of different bosses. It is the beginning of the end of any enterprise when the boss becomes the customer.

Now let's introduce some demonic influences: "It has been decreed from on high that out of every ten employees only two are outstanding and at least two are marginal." *Let the games begin.* If not before, certainly now the customer is forgotten. The gladiators are transfixed on each other. When winners and losers are decreed, who wants to be a loser?

Forced distribution, like grading on a curve, has another pernicious outcome. What if no one were truly outstanding, and the force of custom pushed 20 percent into the "outstanding" category?

I have seen some interesting ploys that reasonable managers have used to deal with forced distributions. One assigned everyone a "4" (the ranking was 1 to 5). The human resources department informed him that his rankings were too high—so he gave everyone a "3." Another called in all his direct reports and explained the company rules: "No more than 20 percent in the top, and 20 percent mandated at the bottom"—whereupon he stated that each of them would be rotated through each category. He then asked them to draw straws for the initial ranking.

Forced ranking is even more pernicious than forced distribution. Yet it has an almost fatal attraction for some companies. I am very close to one such firm; my pleadings notwithstanding, they continue the practice. I was asked to address the 16 most senior officers of another company that is consistently voted among the ten best managed in the country. During the discussion period, I learned that these 16 men (sorry, no women) were ranked similarly—along with others in the executive pool. These were among the most brilliant and effective managers I have ever encountered. Suddenly, the ludicrousness of the situation overcame me. I fell silent—stood and looked at them for a full 60 seconds—then said, "Half of you are below average." Silence again. "I wonder which half." More silence. "I believe it is this half," pointing to the right side of the room. Then addressing the left half, "And half of you are below average," and on and on until only one person remained. I was not asked back.

They did not understand the law of averages—roughly half of any group will be above and half will be below. Or perhaps they believe the radio personality Garrison Keillor when he talks of his hometown, Lake Wobegon, "where every child is above average." I worry that a serious character flaw or a mysterious blind spot robs me of the ability to rank an R&D director against a manufacturing vice president against the CFO against the MIS manager against the vice president of manufacturing and the director of human resources. If I were ranking for succession purposes and were selecting the next CEO, I might wonder if the company needed someone with a strong financial background. If she or he did not have that, is someone in place to make up for the shortfall? It seems that the job should help define the candidate.

Earlier I posed the question: "How do we reward and motivate?" My comments on what not to do regarding pay confirm my belief that merit pay, after base needs and market parity are met, is not an important motivator. Therefore, if there is a 5 percent pay increase pool, everybody gets 5 percent, and we all get back to work. Remember, the marketplace has established the base pay differential. Why complicate our lives and create discontent? The savings in transaction costs far outweigh disgruntlement of those who feel they should have received more than the others. This leads to two other issues tied in with flat versus differential pay increases—slackers and stars. I am some-times asked: "What do we do about those who are not pulling their weight and who receive the same pay increases as the oth-ers?" My quick answer is: "Where is management?" My more studied answer adds: "Peer pressure will help take care of it." The presumption here is that everyone is pulling on the same set of oars, that there are shared goals among the employees and the company. If these goals are not shared, pay alone will not solve the problem.

Effectiveness of peer pressure is captured in this anecdote told to me by Stanley Klion, executive-in-residence at the Columbia Business School, about a gasket company that distrib-uted bonuses as a uniform percentage of annual pay to every-one in the firm. The firm is located in north Chicago—a tough area—and its employees are, for the most part, from minority groups. The company had hired a new employee who clearly was not pulling his weight—and was not even trying. No one from management said a word to the employee. This went on for several weeks, whereupon one day, a 6-foot-4-inch, 250-pound employee walked up to the offender, took a firm hold of his shirt front, got right in his face and said, "Man, you're mess-ing with my profits." The language has been cleaned up for family audiences, but the moral is clear. The offender, by the way, drew his pay and left the firm. Managers who say that they cannot manage without differential pay exhibit an unseem-ly powerlessness, when in fact they have many tools along with peer pressure to help them manage effectively.

As for the stars, the company is sometimes better off without them, if pay is their only motivator. Although their individual performance might be stellar, they are the ones who often throw a monkey wrench in the system. Bending to their needs sometimes acts to the detriment of the firm. In some instances, the right leadership can bring the stars into the company's orbit. This leads to a contradiction to the foregoing argument. In some instances, superperformers will emerge who, over time and in many ways are clearly outliers in the distribution curve of the people of the firm. These performers are usually universally recognized. Paying them more than the firm's nominal scale is probably a true reflection of market value and does not usually create a corrosive jealousy among other members of the firm.

Back again to the question: How do we reward and motivate people? The answer is the same. Pay them at market or better, but don't expect pay alone to reward and motivate. Indeed, reward the whole human being. Carefully apply the comprehensive compensation package proposed here.

Differential incentive pay is a special case of merit pay and deserves the same fate. It should be eliminated. If the company does well and 20 percent of base pay is available for distribution, everyone should get 20 percent—slackers, stars, and all. When differential incentives are used as a reward tool, the dysfunctional artifacts of mistrust that have already been discussed always come into play. The total cost of administering differential incentive plans is greater than the perceived benefits. Appendix A contains some short cases that I use to caricature the problems associated with incentive pay.

3. Promote thoughtfully and carefully.

An important part of the compensation package is to be well-led by those whom you respect and trust or to be followed by those who earnestly support your leadership.

There will always be leaders and followers, but in this world of knowledge workers and technical specialists, the roles are often blurred, sometimes reversed. Furthermore, even during troubled economic periods, workers in the twentieth and twenty-first centuries are more mobile than they were when "command and control" was imprinted on managerial behavior. Today's high cost of turnover and the hidden cost of "soldiering," which is difficult to detect in complex intellectual activity, highlights the importance of leadership selection. Traditional promotion screens—reviews of recent performance ratings and interviews with recent supervisors— usually do not tell us enough about the prospective appointee's ability to synthesize complex situations, to conceptualize so that the task will be clearly understood by others, or to motivate so that people will earnestly wish to achieve their goals. Even these abilities are not enough, however. The leader for today and tomorrow should be able to assist employees when they hit dead ends—to suggest methods and procedures for improvement. In this regard, the leader must possess or be qualified to quickly gain the specific knowledge of the roles he or she is supervising.

Moreover, as I have said before, leaders must understand the system in which they work. Improvement of a system's performance rarely results from an adjustment of one component without a corresponding adjustment to other components. Therefore, leaders must not only have the power to bridge these components or functions, they also need to understand their relationships. In addition, the effective leader should have high energy, the courage to take reasonable risks, and an abiding curiosity, which leads to continuous improvement of the leader's skills as well as the performance of those supervised.

These leadership qualifications are not quickly acquired nor easily discerned. Accordingly, the ideal appointee will have been observed and evaluated over a long period in a variety of roles—not by remote decision makers who rely on written reports and numerical ratings but by those with whom the prospect has worked. Although the promotion decision is clearly management's domain, it should be made with the advice and hopefully the consent of the majority of those whom the appointee will be leading, as well as peers, immediate superiors, other managers, previous subordinates, and internal as well as external customers. This is not a call for an election, however. Business organizations are not democratic institutions, even though they seem sometimes to be awash in politics. Rather, promotion calls for the managerial paradigm described throughout this book: thoughtful, involved, knowledgeable, caring, but tough-minded and courageous leaders who know the people and the methods, policies, and procedures of the tasks they are supervising.

4. Hire carefully and thoughtfully.

Hiring decisions have such profound impact on a company's short- and long-term performance that it could be said, only partially in jest, that the final act of hiring should be consummated in a church, synagogue, or mosque—and only after a searching, arduous courtship. I am particularly in mind of a time when I was best man at a wedding; and a tall, powerfully built Episcopalian priest turned the guests' knees to jelly when he thundered, "Those whom God hath joined together, let no man put asunder!" No, I am not in favor of business indenturement "til death do us part," nor am I in favor of guaranteed lifetime employment. I am in favor of conditions which foster the opportunity for lifetime employment if desired by both parties.

We have created a tragic mess by hiring thoughtlessly when times were good and firing thoughtlessly when times got tough, or if "the person just did not work out." Yet, we bemoan the thought that "there's no loyalty anymore." Similarly, we have job applicants who have no intention of staying long enough to pay out their hiring and training costs or who plan to use the job only as a way station or stepping stone. Both of these behaviors demonstrate disrespect, foster mistrust, and create waste.

Hiring carefully and thoughtfully means, for the employer, making a careful projection of future employment needs, having a contingency plan if trouble arises, having the ability to cross-train or reassign if necessary. Careful hiring also means thorough, hard-nosed, tough-minded interviewing of job applicants by potential coworkers as well as managers. A bad hiring decision costs much more than the person's salary. And it is difficult to reverse. Avoiding mistakes as well as optimizing decisions means checking references and administering tests for traits as well as skills, even though these are of dubious value unless conducted by professionals with modest expectations. It also means much more than assessing skills, abilities, and knowledge, all of which are important but which alone are insufficient. Careful hiring means assessment of the candidate's ability to work in your environment with your coworkers. It does not mean that the candidate should be a clone. Diversity is a virtue—but diversity should foster creative contention, not corrosive stress. The candidate should be apprised of your high expectations, and should be emotionally, physically, and intellectually prepared to meet the criteria for promotion that were discussed earlier.

5. Produce a quality product or service.

It's worth a lot to me to say, "I teach at Columbia Business School." My colleagues are world leaders in research and teaching. The school's administrators are diligent professionals. My students are brilliant, hard-working, independent thinkers. They offer challenges and stimulation every day. I would not want the dean to know it, but I would work just as hard for 40 percent lower pay—and I wouldn't think of leaving. I have colleagues from other fine schools who have similar justifiable pride. Others, not so fortunate, teach at institutions that use their business schools as cash producers and will not make the commitments required to produce quality education.

A critically important part of the compensation package is the institution's commitment to excellence. Time was when people were not very happy to admit that they worked for Ford or Chrysler. Thankfully, that is changing. As president of Ford Motor Company, Donald Peterson was one of the leaders of the change. His decision to delay the introduction of the first Ford Taurus cost the company a lot of money that year. But the car's bugs had not been worked out. Peterson had been preaching "quality" to Ford employees since 1981. His own credibility and his employees' commitment to excellence would have been tarnished had he knowingly permitted defective cars to be sold.

Just as executives inventory their goods, they should conduct an inventory of their commitment to excellence. Have they knowingly released a poor-quality product or service to meet a financial target? Have they looked the other way as they imposed conditions on associates which made it impossible to commit to excellence? Do they have the organization processes in place to ensure quality? If my company conducted annual employee morale surveys, I would see to it that questions were asked about the employees' perception of the quality of the firm's goods or services.

A manufacturing vice president of a hard-driving results-oriented firm is so concerned that he is not getting correct information that he has "sources" who slip to the phone and say, "George, you'd better get down here. We're shipping defects again." Spies are not a proper surrogate for organizational processes that allow commitment to excellence, and George knows that. He is working to improve the processes, but in the meantime he wants to leave no doubt about his commitment.

6. Remove from the organization swiftly and summarily anyone who overtly violates trust.

More specifically, the continued presence of a person who has been found to lie, steal or cheat, or commit other acts which clearly demonstrate dishonesty or lack of integrity is destructive. This book has enumerated the substantial benefits to an organization that is built on trust. These benefits are essentially nullified if leadership knowingly tolerates untrustworthy behavior. Everyone else in the organization will revert to the protective artifices that foster complexity and create waste. I am aware that the assessment of integrity is a complex ethical issue which itself could be the subject of a book. My stipulation here pertains to the person who blatantly transgresses—where there is very little uncertainty about an action. Heartless as it may sound, I make very few allowances for the motivations of the transgressor. The diagnosis might explain untrustworthy behavior but, in my view, does not excuse it. More difficult is the transgression that is harder to diagnose. If the suspicion seems reasonable, the person should be confronted directly. Unless the suspicion is dispelled, the person should be told that he or she has one foot out the door and the other on a banana peel. Again, a society lubricated by trust is damaged if untrustworthy actions are condoned or tolerated. This rule should apply to everyone—from a CEO to hourly workers, customers, and suppliers.

7. If people, making good faith efforts, do not perform satisfactorily, find out why. Reassign or retrain them. If unsuccessful, remove them from the organization—with dignity and respect.

Part of the compensation package is the knowledge that one will be treated fairly if things do not go well. Dealing with the person who, over time, working in good faith, cannot perform the job correctly or who seems unable to be trained to perform other jobs, is a difficult leadership task. The organization needs confidence that leaders are sensitive to the parity between the organization and the individual. If removal of a person who is trying, but not succeeding, seems unfair or poorly handled, the survivors are apt to say, "There but for the grace of God go I." Then if they revert to protective behavior, the system suffers, nullifying any benefits contemplated by the termination. Moreover, the decisions rarely meet unanimous acclaim. Here, the leader must hear the voice of everyone—not just special pleaders or those who are closest. Less difficult but sensitive nevertheless is removal of the person who does not seem to try or who is overtly disruptive to the organization. A reasonable effort should be made to find out why and help remediate the cause, with the caveat that a business organization is not a psychiatric hospital. However, this unhappy situation reflects either a hiring mistake or a change in the person during employment. So the firm has more than a passing responsibility to handle the situation with dignity and respect. Perverse as it sounds, terminations sometimes are clearly morale builders for the survivors. I have terminated middle managers to the applause of the entire organization. "It's about time," I have been told, "that someone saw through that bum." However, termination of a person who has the respect of the organization always heightens unproductive behavior. My colleague, Joel Brockner, offers valuable advice about the "survivor syndrome" in his article in the *California Management Review*.[6] Professor Brockner's research shows that if the survivors believe that the process was unfair, if the pain was not shared by executives and managers, and if communication was thoughtless and poorly conceived, survivor morale and productivity suffered as well. Also important was the perceived value of the termination package. However, one of Professor Brockner's more interesting findings was that the termination package alone did not enhance survivor morale. Companies that ignore the first three criteria might as well save their money if they are concerned about survivor morale. Professor Brockner's research also demonstrates that a morale *boost* was possible if all the actions above were taken properly.

At the risk of sounding avuncular, I suggest that being fired is not the end of the world. Self-serving as it sounds, it might be good for both the employee and the firm. I have been fired, and even though time demonstrated that I was fired unfairly, I had to work through the anger, even hatred and despair, turning them to resolution. Time also demonstrated that being fired was the best thing that could have happened to me. The surviving leaders were determined to run the company into the ground, and they succeeded.

Hiring and firing connotes power, which calls for responsibility. Responsibility connotes thoughtfulness and care, which suggests that the leaders seek advice and consent. Sometimes, however, the leader has information or orders that others might not be aware of. Sometimes, the leader is at liberty to share that intelligence with others, sometimes not. In order to build trust in the organization, leaders should err on the side of disclosure if they err at all. But the final decision should be the leaders' within the confines of the law. The decision is not, and should not be, a democratic one; nor should it be unduly affected by external factors such as trade unions or government pressure. The body politic shuns tough decisions and rarely makes good ones. That's what leaders are for. The leader who is timid and indecisive is a less effective custodian of the system and has less chance of gaining the trust of its constituencies than does the leader who is decisive in protecting the system—not just the components. All these complexities are intensified by the realization that businesses are people. Their needs are interrelated. Their roles are symbiotic, although not always congruent.

8. Share the pain.

When times are tough, the pain should be shared. First to go should be the nonpersonnel expenses—especially executive perks. These cuts should be communicated as actions that are necessary to preserve the organization's most precious assets—its people. R&D and important capital expenditures, however, should be preserved as long as possible if the company expects to emerge from the downturn with the ability to compete. Next is executive pay. It should be cut before personnel are terminated. These cuts carry some risk. Executives are people, too. They may have big mortgages and youngsters in college, so they might decide to leave if the cuts are too severe. To the extent that the economic downturn occurred on their watch, however, they have a share of the responsibility for assisting in the turnaround. Those who leave for greener pastures may be missed temporarily, but as a turnaround manager I have been impressed at the ability of others to fill the gaps created by the departure of those who have been considered irreplaceable.

Although dollar savings from executive pay cuts rarely make the difference between survival or death, they are symbolically important. The alienation that occurs when pain is not shared by the executive suite can lead to enormous productivity loss at a time when a company most needs the unfettered commitment of everyone. On the day following a large company's announcement that hundreds of people would be terminated, it announced a 32 percent increase in pay for its CEO. He does not have a prayer of turning the company around. His support evaporated on the day that the pay increase was announced.

A young professional woman recounted to me how the owner of a small company she worked for called everyone together the week before Christmas to explain the layoff of five employees and to explain why there would be no bonuses that year. The day after Christmas he showed up in a new luxury vehicle. It will be a miracle if the business survives. Although these are examples of gross mismanagement, their permutations are all too evident in other troubled companies. Precious few products or sales are made around the office water cooler.

9. Share the rewards with everyone in the system.

The advice to pay at market or better introduced the idea that bonuses should make up a portion of monetary compensation. This section will support the argument previously made that everyone, not just the few, should participate. The supporting theory is that no part of a system is more important than another. Certainly, some parts might be more difficult to replace than others. One job might require a broader range of skills than another—or more education and training. Some jobs might be more difficult and more dangerous to perform. These facts of life are acknowledged when pay is set by the marketplace. But they do not address other verities: Failure of a $2-dollar gasket can ruin a $10,000 engine; a rude telephone operator can destroy months of painstaking customer prospecting. A disinterested customer service representative can cause the defection of a valued client.

Two years ago, I was asked by the students at Columbia Business School to participate in their annual musical production called "The Follies." During dress rehearsal, they discarded much of what they may have learned about job functions, chain of command, and channels of communication. They "fell to" with a refreshing sense of purpose. When the electrician was swamped, they helped out. Actors became stagehands when necessary. The director, who I proudly noted was one of my students, orchestrated the melange to perfection. She was clearly the leader—but the leader in the sense of coordinating, integrating, augmenting the general understanding of the sense of purpose—not barking commands or micromanaging. The production was a roaring success. The rewards were not only a standing ovation but the sense of bond among cast members that will last throughout their lives. I hope that the lessons in organizational process and systems theory will last as long.

Among those lessons are these: If the lights had gone out or if the spotlight had been trained on the pianist instead of the singer, the performance would have been diminished. If the stagehand had pulled the curtain at the wrong time, if the pianist had missed a cue, if an important prop had disappeared, or if a member of the chorus had missed a cue, the leading roles would have been tarnished. Or if the lead performers had pushed and shoved to upstage one another, or stepped on one another's lines, the production would have been a shambles.

No different in the workaday world. The soldering defect in my $1500 cellular telephone plagued me for a year before the problem was diagnosed, giving me the opportunity to swear at the phone and the company—not always under my breath. The phone's marvelous design and excellent engineering were made dross by a simple manufacturing defect. The phone has now been replaced and all is well—almost.

During a visit to General Motors, one of its executives convinced me that I should buy an Oldsmobile Bravada. Manhattan has no Oldsmobile dealership, so I went to New Jersey. Just before writing the check, I asked about service. The dealer pointed to the bus stop, indicating that I could take the bus back to Manhattan while the car was being serviced. In the line of sight of the bus stop, just two blocks away, was a Ford dealership. Within an hour, I was the owner of a Ford Explorer. The Ford dealer offered pick-up service or a "loaner." I am enjoying the Ford but probably would have enjoyed the Oldsmobile. All the design, engineering, manufacturing and marketing of the Oldsmobile Bravada—down the drain because of a dealer.

The foregoing is not to suggest that we use bonuses as bribes for good work. Rather, to create a sense of belonging, to symbolize that although base pay and positions might be different, everyone is important. The pride engendered by this symbol redounds to both the system and the individual. Properly structured, it creates a productive symbiosis, not merely a negative covenant. Not "I can't do well unless the system does, so I'll do what I have to do." But, "the system's success is mine also. What else can I do to contribute?"

And this brings us back full circle. The whole human being, not just economic man, shows up for work. The bonus pay can be both extrinsic and intrinsic. It rewards the economic man and carries the promise that the whole human being will be rewarded. But pay alone will not deliver the promise. The other components of compensation are equally important: Treating people with respect, hiring and promoting thoughtfully and carefully, producing a quality product or service, and taking action to preserve the system are intrinsic to compensation. If you wish to buy performance with bonuses alone, save your money.

The concept of symbiosis enlightens the decision about the size of the bonuses or if they should be paid at all. The superordinate priority is the long-term health of the system.

When the system is a business organization, reinvestment is usually required. Some reinvestment is necessary to maintain the status quo, more is required for growth. After reinvestment needs come the other constituencies. Debt must be served. Equity should be served, either with market-competitive dividends or growth in value, or a reasonable combination of both. Taxes serve government needs, and contributions in effort or money can serve the eleemosynary needs. Balance is required—balance which is decided by constituencies of goodwill whose aim is to preserve and grow the system while making a contribution to society. When one of these constituencies maximizes its position, the system suffers. Punishing wages and onerous work rules have destroyed many businesses' ability to compete. More recently, excessive debt requirements have had similar effect, although much of this has been prompted by equity holders seeking to maximize their position by using excessive leverage. Many of them have ended up with 100 percent of nothing. Avaricious, unchecked management groups also have taken their toll. Punishing taxes in return for deteriorating services have driven businesses out of New York City. The concept of maximizing shareholder value, which plays out as though equity were the only stakeholder, has had similar disastrous effect. Maximization is a system's biggest enemy—if it is directed at any individual component.

If this book is about anything, it is about the power of a system whose components are singularly fixed on a common goal—where adversarial relationships and the attendant transaction costs are submerged in pursuit of that goal, where all people in the system feel that they are recognized and fairly rewarded for their efforts—because the system will thrive; jobs will be preserved, people will be well paid; debt, equity, and society will be richly served.

10. Provide leadership that fosters trust.

The suggestions offered here should provide a foundation for trust. In addition, leaders should praise the messenger who brings bad news, especially if the messenger has made an attempt to rectify a problem he or she has recognized. *Communication* is a fuzzy, often misused word. But when communication provides access to useful, actionable information up, down, and across the organization, and when communication is offered without fear of ill-feeling or reprisal, problems will surface and solutions will be found that otherwise would be submerged in a melange of political activities and bureaucratic nonsense.

6
Measurements

For years, I have criticized the shibboleth, "If it ain't broke, don't fix it." The manifestation of that management maxim has contributed mightily to our economic decline and undermines the importance of constant improvement, causing us to wait too late to protect our markets. Now we have another shibboleth almost as dangerous: "If you can't measure it, you can't manage it." We have an army of clerks playing Solomon, measuring trivia—thus masking the importance of those measurements that are critical to the health of the enterprise. Certainly, some measurements are absolutely necessary; however, others measure the wrong things, focusing our attention away from critical issues. In sum, the cost of gathering and reacting to measurements is a significant portion of a firm's administrative costs. More frightening, we no longer trust the measurements we receive, so we ignore them or use artifices to get around them. Even more frightening, the company can make decisions that will put it out of business when the decisions are made on the basis of wrong information.

Consider the U.S. automobile industry. One of the industry's biggest mistakes was to measure costs in minute detail. (However, most cost measurements use allocations which mask the true costs.) But when the industry tried to measure the benefits in this same minute detail, it lost sight of the big picture. For instance, many incremental improvements that require additional capital or increased expenses do not normally meet the hurdle rates set by our financial departments. While we were marching to our paradigm, the Japanese marched right into our markets by constantly improving their cars during the 1970s and 1980s, regardless of detailed hurdle rate calculations.[1] Some of the improvements were not immediately noticeable. For example, the transmissions of their automobiles improved year by year. Vibration and noise were reduced. Responsiveness got better and better. Similar incremental improvements were made in engines, chassis, and bodies. Then the interiors, and the fit and finish. For all these, we in Detroit might have been able to measure the cost, but the Japanese were thinking of the benefits.

How do we measure the costs to us and the benefits to them of that fateful day in the 1970s when the collective consciousness of the U.S. car-buying public swung over to the conclusion that Japanese cars were okay? No longer were Japanese cars just for liberal college professors and wacko environmentalists. Now anyone would be proud to drive one. Indeed the new cachet was Japanese—U.S.-made cars were for Archie Bunker. Too late for us then! The floodgates were open. We would spend the next quarter century trying to regain our prestige. We are reversing the trend in the 1990s but may never regain our market share.

But none of this loss was for the lack of measurements. Detroit was Valhalla for bean counters. Net present value, discounted cash flow, cost-benefit analysis, machine utilization, variance from standard, direct labor and material productivity—you name it, they measured it. More than anything else, they measured costs, albeit incorrectly, as activity-based and resource-based accounting have demonstrated. And, to make it worse, cost improvements were addressed after the design was set—too late then. The big cost savings are taken care of in the design, not managed after the fact.

But even if the direct costs were approximately right, they were irrelevant if the cars did not sell. A critical element of the discounted cashflow analysis is the revenue line. A committee of poets, painters, and tarot card readers might have had greater success than Detroit measurement mavens in predicting the effect of Japanese competition on our sales.

Great leaders have always known this. Great companies have always practiced it. They suffer the ministrations of the minutiae men, but they rise above them and "do the right thing." They keep the customer sharply in focus, even if the benefits of that focus cannot be measured in dollars and cents.

"Whoa!" you say. "It's precisely this type of entrepreneurial irresponsibility that gets companies in trouble! Revenues must exceed costs, and cash must be available when needed." Of course. But the great leaders and great companies also know their basic cost drivers sufficiently well to make informed decisions, even if the information is not included in their financial reports and their capital-budgeting criteria.

Building Trust in Our Measurements

I said earlier that some measurements are critically important. These are the ones we should focus on. One way to determine whether the measurements are worth doing is to answer the following questions:

Exactly what is being measured?

When?

By whom?

For what purpose?

By what method?

Is the time order of data preserved?

How is the measure to be communicated?

How will measurement affect the activity being measured?

Have we measured costs but neglected the benefits?

Have we kept the customer in view?

If we do not understand the measurements we use, it follows that we should not trust them. Unfortunately, when we do understand them, we sometimes trust them even less. Ironically, in order to trust our measurements, we must first mistrust them. We cannot responsibly accept them at face value. They are a result of assumptions, hypotheses, sampling techniques, methods of measurement, and techniques of presentation. Measurements come to us as a result of prior classification, simplification, and aggregation. They are symbols merely—shorthand to help us cut through complexity to make informed decisions and take reasonable actions.

When we do not understand that they are merely symbols, we risk disaster. Many business tragedies are the result of actions based on inappropriate, incorrect, or misleading information from flawed measurements: measurement of profits while ignoring cash; measurement of assets at book rather than at market value; measurement of product, but not customer, profitability; measurement of product profitability by allocating overhead as a multiple of direct labor costs; measurement of variances from standard rather than acknowledging that standards should not be fixed in time but should highlight opportunity for improvement; measurement of share of market even though the market is being redefined by indirect competition.

I have seen CEOs lulled into ignoring the balance sheet by focusing on operating statements. These CEOs were incredulous when the bank pulled the plug or when the board of directors asked for their resignations. One CEO who confidently told his board in April, "We'll never have a cash problem," was scrambling in August to replace a $20 million line of credit which he had taken for granted. As the cash eroded, the bank became nervous and then exacerbated the problem by pulling its line. The CEO was watching the operating statement but relied on his CFO's cash projections, which were extrapolations of the past, not careful projections based on current information.

Fortunately, our measurements serve us well in many instances. Indeed, when the components that are being measured interact in random fashion to form a system under statistical control, we can make reasonably good predictions from our measurements. But as responsible decision makers, we must first be able to discern whether the measurements form such a system; and second, we must understand enough about each of the components and the nature of their interactions that we are able to assist in the improvement of the system.

No manager, therefore, should take action as a result of a measurement that she or he does not fully understand. This does not mean that, at every decision point, managers should resurrect all the raw data that supports the aggregate measurement. It does mean that managers should have a current understanding of the elements and processes that are used to produce the measurements. This type of understanding is a journey with no end. A manager in a new assignment should seize the opportunity to question deeply every measurement that crosses his or her desk. More time consuming, but just as important: Every manager who has been at the same job for more than a year should carefully review her or his understanding of the measurements that trigger decisions and actions. "Whitney's dumb and stupid act" is an approach that I have found to be effective. My calumnious colleagues have observed that this artifice, which seems natural when it comes from me, might be more difficult for others to employ. But when confronted with a measurement I do not understand, I now ask, "Can you help me? I'm not sure just what you mean when you say that our cost of goods is less than our competitor's. Maybe if you can help me understand how we measure our cost of goods and how they measure theirs, I can make a better decision." Of course, I have just opened Pandora's box. The calculation of cost of goods, particularly for a manufactured product, is one of the more complex business exercises. If the decision maker truly understands all the components of cost of goods, then obviously there is no need to embark on this tortuous journey. But far too often decision makers do not really understand how cost of goods or other business measures are derived. They only think they understand. At least once a year, every manager should cast off the mantle of wisdom, assume Whitney's slack-jawed countenance, and begin asking dumb questions. Then when a manager makes decisions and takes action, she or he can do so with some assurance.

Earlier, I maligned the bean counters who focused on cost data, sometimes to the detriment of the revenue line. That was not to imply that costs are unimportant. When costs are stated, however, we should know or be able quickly to find out their components. The aggregation of data into a single numerical indicator often masks useful information. For instance, the alleged components of cost of goods vary widely from firm to firm, sometimes from plant to plant within the same firm. Although most capture direct labor and direct material costs uniformly, allocated costs may, in one instance, be assigned to cost of goods and, in another instance, to SG&A (selling, general, and administrative). Yet decision makers, particularly those whose training is primarily financial, tend to look at an operating statement and muse, "Seems that cost of goods is okay" without really knowing whether COGS is too low or SG&A too high—or whether both are too low or both too high. Adding to the uncertainty are depreciation and amortization. A fully depreciated plant may appear to be more profitable than a new one, yet it may be a festering sore, soon to create serious profit or cash problems.

Of course, the cost of goods is disaggregated as it travels down the organization chart. Operators will generally have more information about cost components than their supervisors, but even for operators, the allocations will mask useful information. This is confirmed by the vigorous debates sparked by allocation discussions. As many companies have learned to their sorrow, allocation decisions that are driven by accounting conventions and that focus on inventory costs and ignore SG&A cost drivers usually do not reflect the true product profitability.

As a manager of turnarounds and troubled companies, I try to follow the rule, "Feed the winners and starve the losers."[2] When resources are strained, they must be wisely deployed. Sound as this policy may seem, it is difficult to discriminate between winners and losers because traditional cost accounting focuses on inventory costing and does not reflect the total costs, which also include development, marketing, administrative, distribution, servicing, warranty, return processing, and the entire package associated with product profitability. In most troubled companies, I find that managers have not known their true costs, and have accordingly concentrated their effort on precisely the wrong products. The same is true of services, where direct costs are usually fairly well tracked but administrative cost allocations have been woodenly applied and have masked the total costs of delivering the service. In addition, knowledge of all the cost drivers can help managers understand which customers are profitable. In many firms that I have studied, half of their customers are unprofitable. This does not necessarily mean that all those customers should be dropped. But it clearly delineates a problem that needs to be addressed.

Measuring Six Sigma and Zero Defects

I have long been an admirer of the Motorola Corporation. Its heroic efforts in the world's most complex and competitive arenas have been an inspiration. Managers at Motorola whom I have talked to ascribe much of their success to the famous "Six Sigma" endeavor. Six Sigma, as Motorola uses it, refers to the goal of fewer than 3.4 defects per million units produced. Under this banner, the company has made remarkable progress. Indeed, Robert Galvin, chairman of the Executive Committee, stated that Motorola can soon achieve the goal of no defects.[3] Japanese manufacturers have made similar comments.

Not to belittle Six Sigma and Zero Defect endeavors, but to gain better understanding, I have asked executives from these firms, "What is a defect?" The usual answer: "Something that does not meet specifications." I have then asked, "Who sets the specifications?" Where their companies were selling to other companies, the answers have been, "The customer specifies." For branded products, they have said that their specifications are usually set by marketing, design, and engineering personnel.

In far too many instances, I have found that specifications have been set by engineers or designers who have not consulted with marketing, manufacturing, suppliers, tool and die makers, and others who are important to the process. Sometimes these specifications are too tight. Sometimes they are not tight enough. Sometimes they do not cover important requirements.

Sadly, I observed one occasion where Six Sigma, according to a company's initial specifications, was not met, whereupon the specifications were "redefined" until Six Sigma could be achieved. On that occasion, I happened to agree that the specifications were too tight for the purpose for which they were intended, but it brought me squarely back to the question, "What is a defect?" What measurements should be used to determine whether something is defective? Then, these musings brought me back to the problem of single-number measurements, and ratios (Six Sigma), to the problem of tying rewards and recognition to such measurements, and to the problem of oversimplifying the measurements of complex operations. In this spirit of complexity, let me attempt to clarify the preceding conundrum by complicating it. To begin, most of us should agree that meeting specifications is the beginning of the journey, not the end. Many of our domestic manufacturers have been eclipsed in part because we have set specifications at tolerances that we were confident of meeting at the time—and we have been content to live at those specifications. Meanwhile, in our automobile example, our competitors, using the idea of continuous improvement, have inexorably tightened their specifications. Moreover, when they achieved perfection, they raised the bar. My friend Kosaku Yoshida observes, "If we can meet Six Sigma, perhaps our specifications are not tight enough; and if we truly believed in continuous improvement, we would continue to tighten the specifications."

Next complication: Most of us, in the quest for quality, have heard of Taguchi's loss function. Taguchi's hypothesis has two ramifications: As a process produces results near the target, performance losses become almost infinitesimal—perhaps so small that we need not worry about them. But as results approach the outer specification limits, the performance losses expand geometrically. So, if Taguchi is right, we could have a product that meets the specifications, but within those tolerances produce a wide variance in results. Let's complicate things even further. Our zeal might cause us to specify—not too tightly—but improperly. Defects in steel that is used to manufacture precision instruments would not be classified as defects in steel that is used for construction. Of course these differences are prescribed by the design and in the specifications, but an indiscriminate quest for zero defects can unnecessarily drive up costs. And the coup de grace is Dr. Deming's observation that a fixation on zero defects may direct our attention away from the customer. If the customer does not want the product or service or cannot use it, the goal of zero defects is irrelevant.

In the context of the foregoing, let's take a balanced view of Six Sigma and Zero Defects. To the extent that these goals provide a motivation for improvement of quality, they are useful. To the extent that they are a source of pride, they are salutary. To the extent that they are woodenly applied, they can blind us to customer needs, can mask important information, and can drive up costs. To the extent that these goals are used in the system of reward and recognition, they can lead to irrational behavior. It is imperative, therefore, that we use these tools for information, not for individual reward, and it is imperative that when we do use them, we understand what we are measuring.

Measurement of Distribution Center Service Levels

For several years, our review meetings at the supermarket chain included a report on service levels. "We hit 94 percent last week," or "Only 92 percent this week. We've got to crack some heads." As reports were made, I would nod wisely and go on to the next agenda item. Shame on me! Not until I began getting complaints from the stores did I realize that reported service levels not only were bad, they were largely irrelevant. The reported service level measured only the "in-stock" position of items that the store ordered from the distribution center. The service levels did not measure late deliveries, which caused overtime work for store personnel. Service levels did not measure wrong selections and misdirected pallets. They did not measure dented cans and other damages caused by the distribution process. They did not measure the effect on both the distribution center and the stores of two trucks arriving at the store's receiving dock at the same time. Downtime for the trucks and drivers! Confusion, overtime, and diversion of employees from customer service to unloading trucks! But our service levels were in the 90s! Comforted by that intelligence, we failed to understand or improve the system until our store managers complained. Our store managers were captive customers. What if they had been free to choose?

Measurements of Piece Work

Yes, piece work is alive, but not always well—not only in ghetto sweat shops or third-world countries, but also in "modern" industrial operations in the United States. A large manufacturing facility of one of our giant corporations ties part of its workers' pay to a productivity figure which is driven by numbers, types of operations performed, and pieces produced. The managers aver that this method of pay is mandated by the union. Perhaps! But if it is mandated, it is because trust has taken a holiday. The employees do not trust the company to pay fairly, and the company does not trust the employees to put forth their best efforts. Harry Levinson's jackass fallacy again! But trust is not alone in taking a holiday. Quality might be among the missing, also. "But we can take care of that," one might say. "We will not pay for defective pieces." Another journey of Sisyphus. How do we define quality? Then how do we identify poor quality? Inspectors, of course! Suspicion intensifies. The inspectors, who are also members of the union, are asked to penalize their "brothers and sisters." Worse, they might be coopted by the system and reduce their vigilance. But these are not all the costs. A veritable army of accountants and industrial engineers is required to count the pieces and assign piece rates. These become the source of endless wrangling between the shop stewards and managers. Piece rates become the centerpiece of the annual contract negotiations. And there is more! Workers who are assigned to a job with a particular piece rate cannot be assigned to a job with a higher piece rate unless adjustments are made to their hourly rates. Bring on the accountants again—and the supervisors, and the shop steward, and the industrial engineers. Here's what makes this situation even more ludicrous: The workers can produce only the number of pieces that the production schedule calls for. Still more ludicrous, direct labor is only 6 percent of the cost. If the company were to use the workers' last year's pay as a base and then add 15 percent across the board in order to buy out of these destructive work rules, production, quality, and morale would improve. Administrative and accounting costs would decrease much more than the pay increment. Profits would soar.

There are notable exceptions to piece work problems, of course. Lincoln Electric, one of the best manufacturing companies in the world, pays its workers on the basis of piece work. Moreover, the workers who make the grade—not all do—like it. They earn big multiples of their counterparts in industry. Perhaps pay for piece work is the major reason for Lincoln Electric's success. But my study of the company suggests that the fact that there are very few management layers, that most of the managers have come through the ranks, that the workers are involved in creating and implementing work improvement methods, and that workers have a forum in which to air their complaints are also factors. Perhaps most important is the intense pride the workers have in themselves, in their work, and in their company.

In one U.S. company that I visited, piece work not only raised supervisory costs and lowered quality but had caused measurement activities to run amok. There were 1100 piece rates, each of which required adjustment by an industrial engineer as the process changed and as annual wage reviews were made. I was told, but was not able to verify, that 600 industrial engineers and accountants were employed by the company and that more than half of these were involved in managing piece rates.

Measurements and Benchmarking

Supermarkets for years compared operating results with similar noncompeting companies. Indeed, most industry associations provide this form of benchmarking for their members. Benchmarking is potentially one of the most useful concepts we have developed in recent years. But like so many others, it can backfire when used improperly. Numerical benchmarking can create more questions than answers. For example, a determined chairman of a supermarket chain's holding company who believed in managing with numerical measurements returned from a benchmark meeting with the mandate that from this day forward, at this organization, the shrinkage in gross margin would be 1 percent or less—or there would be no bonuses this year. He supported his position with the observation that "Chain Y on the West Coast has 1 percent shrink and so can we." Panic! Our shrink was greater than 2 percent. And we were doing everything we knew to keep it down. Of course a task force was formed, and of course telephone calls began speeding across the continent. The first discovery from this frantic activity was that Chain Y had built into their shrink reporting a 2 percent allowance for meat, fruits, vegetables, and other perishable items. Inasmuch as these items contributed about 30 percent of the total sales, 0.6 percent was accounted for. In addition, Chain Y reduced its measured shrink by the amount of rebates from manufacturers for certain promotions, dented cans, damaged cartons, and unsalable merchandise. The benchmarking chain did not book these allowances against reported shrinkage. Rather, it took them in as income and credited them to a special account. This finding contributed to another 0.2 percent. Similar disparities were found. By the time all bookkeeping adjustments were made, the shrink numbers were the same for both firms. Management accounting and telephone costs went up, however, because of the time it took to chase the numbers and make the comparisons. Firms should always try to learn from others but should avoid blindly adapting another company's practices without understanding how those practices can be usefully integrated in the company's own methods, practices, policies, and values. More to the point, however, companies should avoid reliance on single-number indicators unless they are prepared to conduct a detailed analysis of how the number is derived.

Net Interest Margin—a Measurement Oversimplification

Commercial banks can now testify to the danger of oversimplified measurements. For years, their trusted talisman was the net interest margin: income from interest plus fees from all sources less outgo for all expenses as well as cost of capital. Lowell L. Bryan's book, *Breaking Up the Bank*, argued that this single numeric indicator has served to mask important differences in the profitability of both deposits and loans.[4] The most profitable depositors were the elderly, the upscale consumer, and corporations. Deposits from the first two were profitable because of the relatively low cost of acquiring and keeping their business. Before deregulation, corporations were doubly profitable; interest was not paid on corporate deposits. In addition, the total cost of servicing corporate loans, along with their excellent repayment performance, made corporations the banks' most profitable borrowers. So profitable, in fact, that the larger corporations became aware that they could perform the bank's function by issuing their own debt. Other corporations began to seek financial intermediaries other than commercial banks. Soon, these intermediaries not only had their feet in the door, they were in the kitchen. Had the banks asked themselves this question about net interest margin: "Exactly what is being measured?" and had they responded to the question "How will the information affect the activity being measured?", we might have escaped the banking cataclysm we are witnessing in the 1990s. Proper measurement of sources of income and expenses might not have saved them, but without that measurement they were sailing on angry seas without a compass.

Checklists as Measures of Performance

A store manager in New Jersey showed me his inspection checklist. He was measured on 172 criteria. About half of the measures were binary, the other half scalar—yes or no, or 1 to

10. He was expected to score at least 80 percent on the binary measures and an average of 8 on the scalar measures. The checklist was devised by the operations manager and applied to all the stores in the chain. It was not tailored to the special situations of individual stores. Inspections were made at random by members of the regional staff.

Just prior to one of these random inspections, the store had a fire in the trash compactor, a flood in the basement, and eight of its employees were late to work because the same downpour which flooded the basement had inundated the streets. The indomitable inspector, however, sloshed through the floods. When he arrived, he penalized the store manager because the floor at the front of the store was muddy. The fire in the compactor and the flood in the basement were not on the checklist. If the store manager had used his head, he would have let the store burn down to the water level in the basement. Then he would not have had muddy floors.

Of course, the regional executive conducting the inspection was wrong. A wise supervisor would have removed his coat and tie and asked, "What can I do to help?" Wise or not, the supervisor was also in a bind. He was measured on how many inspections he made in a day.

The flooded store example is a caricature of other uses of measurements, less egregious perhaps, but pervasive and destructive nevertheless. When people are evaluated on criteria over which they have no control, when they are confused by the criteria, or when the criteria are woodenly applied, people are apt to use one of two strategies: dispirited submission or dissimulation—neither of which you would expect to find in a job description. But think of it! Having to score 80 percent "yes" or an average of 8 out of 10 possible, on 172 criteria. Hopeless!

Measurements—Too Many or Too Few?

The store manager example introduces the subject of a lively debate in much of corporate America. Various and sundry experts are now opining that people should be measured and evaluated on no more than four or five criteria—six at the most. Misguided and wrong! When measurements are used for performance evaluation, both are confounded. Wrong also, because it is foolhardy to believe that any complex activity can be described by so few criteria. Wrong also, because conditions change, but the measurement criteria tend to be static. By the end of the evaluation period, the criteria might no longer be relevant.

Misguided, because this line of thinking tends to confuse measurements for purposes of evaluation with measurements which provide information. Indeed, measurements ideally are special cases of information—feedback to help the manager or operator. In this sense, thousands of measurements might be needed. If I were a store manager, I would welcome a long checklist to help me manage—to help me avoid the trap of looking at the same thing every day, perhaps overlooking other tasks important to the store's appearance or readiness. But the checklist would be for my use—not my supervisor's. Moreover, I would tailor it to my store's special needs. Furthermore, I would convene a group of my store employees to help develop the list. Certainly they could add items and insights that I alone would not have. Even more certainly, they would more willingly participate in the fulfillment of expectations that they had helped to create. After the checklist was completed, I might even wish to use it to score myself—to provide a benchmark for further improvement. It is not out of the realm of reason that I might ask my supervisor to use the checklist to "walk me through my store" in hopes that he or she could make suggestions that would help me improve my performance. The heroic assumption here is that the supervisor would have enough knowledge to be of assistance—that the supervisor would not be some well-meaning, fast-track college graduate whose lack of experience would force her or him to use the only resource possible—the wooden use and rigid application of a generic checklist.

Measurements for information are welcomed by workers who want to do a good job. As an inept and cowardly pilot, I worshiped my preflight and landing checklists, which, by the way, utilized more than four or five binary and scalar measures. My only supervisors were myself and my Maker. Inasmuch as I was not ready to meet Him, I welcomed all the help I could get.

Measurements and
Management Accounting

A company I once owned had a client who was justifiably
angry with our performance. Dreading an imminent show-
down, I decided to confront his anger head-on. "Ben," I said,
"We may not be very good"—long pause—"but we sure are
slow"—another pause—"and expensive." I figured that it was
better to start out by agreeing on something. I doubt that my
friends in management accounting would be willing to use the
same ploy, and I am certain they are smarting from my earlier
criticisms of financial accounting. I hope they won't mind terri-
bly that I have a little fun at their expense. After all, I am as
tough on management professors; moreover, I could not have
written this book without making most of the mistakes that I
am so quick to criticize. But, in general, the reports produced
by management accountants are wrong, late, and expensive.
Moreover, the most punishing expenses are not the accountants' salaries and related costs, but rather the untrustworthy
information their profession provides. In their defense, management accountants that I have known try to do the right
thing. But their training, so firmly rooted in the precepts of
financial accounting, and their assigned roles as police, have
rendered them almost useless—if not destructive—to operating
managers. Now, whose fault is all this? Certainly the accountants, as professionals, must share the blame. Every profession
has the duty consistently to improve. But the blame must be
shared by intellectually lazy and derogative senior managers
who have suspected that the information that they were getting
was useless or wrong, and who have done nothing about
it...who have abrogated leadership responsibility by assigning
traffic-cop responsibility to the accountants. The chief culprits,
of course, are we professors, who still teach traditional cost
accounting. But most tenured professors are beyond reach, and
many of the nontenured ones are too timid to make waves. So
again, business will have to make do in spite of the things that
we teach in many business schools.

One does not need to be an accountant to develop information
that is useful to managers. Indeed, the first management

accountants were engineers, and therein lies the heart of my thesis. All management accountants should be fired. Those who have not been permanently damaged by their past training should be rehired and placed directly in an operating unit. Some should become line managers. Because of their experience, they know where the data are. Because they are usually intelligent, they can learn to discriminate between data that are useful and those that are not. Because of their training, they know the rudiments of analysis and can be taught the rudiments of analysis that are useful for decision making. But management accountants should be physically and professionally removed from the financial accounting function.

To underscore the dangers in traditional accounting methods, I present the exercise given in Appendix B to participants in my MBA and executive seminars. It demonstrates the problems of properly assigning SG&A (selling, general, and administrative) costs to products or customer groups, and it dramatizes the untrustworthiness of traditional product cost accounting. Although this exercise deals with manufacturing, similar issues emerge for service businesses and resellers. As practitioners in activity-based costing (ABC) and resource-based accounting have emphasized, allocation formulas and rules of thumb are poor substitutes for measuring and assigning costs and cost drivers to specific products, customers, customer groups, or distribution channels.

More on Standard Costing and Variance Reporting

From time to time, cost accountants and industrial engineers go through the plant to observe the work being done, compare it with other information they might have, and establish standard costs for each activity. Thereafter, variances from these standards are reported. In theory, standard costs are to be updated periodically or whenever a process change occurs. Sometimes this is done on a timely basis; more often it is not. In any event, most variance reporting creates more heat than light—witness the arguments and justifications from plant managers when the monthly variances are reported. In many cases, plant managers do not trust the engineers, accountants, or the numbers.

On some occasions, variance reporting institutionalizes waste. As long as standards are met, why improve? Say there is a standard scrap allowance of 5 percent. Instead of working to get scrap to zero, the tendency is just to meet the standard. Rather than adopt a standard and report variance, I would track previous period performances and work to improve them consistently.

Covering variance deficiencies fosters other aberrant behavior: Manufacturing operations have fought for new product lines, not because they would be truly profitable or enhance corporate strategy, but because the increase in units produced would reduce the amount of overhead allocated to each unit. Rather than cover deficiency, wouldn't it be better to improve the process so that additional costs are reduced, regardless of any standard that might be set? Moreover, even though the unit costs might go down, we probably will institutionalize a tendency to overproduce. To some extent, the pain will have been postponed, but it will not be ameliorated. But because performance seems to improve, everyone could be promoted into better jobs long before the auditors blow the whistles and require a reserve for obsolete inventory. Then, when the new CEO arrives, she or he will be delighted to take the big reserve, which reflects on the departed miscreants. Furthermore, the reserve clears the decks for the new CEO's first year. Thereafter, the dreary process begins again.

We're not through with standards and variances, however. Standards are set not only for the plant as a whole, but for various pieces and parts. A standard is set for a direct laborer's output, for machine utilization, for a specific process output. Then, variances are measured and reported. Forget that standards and variances are permutations of an incorrect premise, and forget how silly it is to measure pieces and parts as if they were independent of each other and the system.

Next, consider the reporting process. Generally, variances are reported at the end of some agreed-upon accounting period—

say, a week, four weeks, or a quarter. By the time they are reported, however, they are history. Of course, a line supervisor could use the negative variance report to beat a worker about the head and shoulders. The supervisor might feel better, but I doubt if the variances would improve.

The artifacts of standard setting and variance reporting are not limited to manufacturing. They can be found in contingency reserves of service and resale businesses. One service firm had a reserve of $15 million for customer complaints and lawsuits. Because the contingency was buried in the cost budget, it became institutionalized. Only when one of the managers lifted this reserve up to constant scrutiny was it addressed. Just one year later, the expenditures were reduced substantially. Other firms use contingency reserves for different purposes. The managers know that various reserves are available. This lulls them sometimes to accept suboptimal performance, knowing that the reserve will bail them out.

If improvement is to be made, it will not be made by producing variance reports. Improvement will come through understanding causes of waste, complexity, and variation, and then addressing those causes. Moreover, causes are not revealed by the most recent data point—last week's variance report. They are revealed in part by analysis of a run chart that plots performance over an appropriate period and notes conditions and special causes. Furthermore, causes of variations will be revealed by those who are doing the work with the timely help of appropriate specialists and technicians.

We are still not through with the problems of variance reporting. There are hundreds more examples, but the one that follows is the pinnacle of folly. The purchasing vice president of a large manufacturing concern was working to establish a value-added supplier program. Dozens of enlightening meetings were held with suppliers. The free, open, creative interchange produced tens of dozens of ideas that dramatically reduced the total cost of manufacturing. In some instances, scrap and rework were reduced and throughput was improved by the purchase of better, sometimes more expensive, raw materials. Even though the materials were more expensive, the company was achieving its overall objective. Total costs were reduced dramatically. One day the purchasing vice president and I were working on a related issue—rewards and recognition. "Joe," I asked, "How are you evaluated?" "On purchase price variance," he replied sadly. Some accounting maven was spending hundreds of hours, tracking previous supplier prices, establishing standards for the year, and setting up a mechanism for tracking variances so that Joe and his colleagues in purchasing could be rewarded or punished accordingly. A fool's errand in the first place. Irrelevant in the second. And third, destructive. The report worked counter to the total low-cost program. Had Joe been looking out for his own hide, he would have sabotaged the value-added supplier program. Instead, he sublimated his own performance evaluations for the good of the firm. Commendable, certainly—but why put people through such *angst*?

When I recount similar examples to senior executives, they express sympathy that such things happen in other companies. Then they pat me on my 65-year-old gray head as if to assure me that it does not happen in their companies. Wrong! This nonsense or its ilk happens in every company. Most executives do not believe it happens on their watch, because they do not listen to the people doing the work. Instead, they talk to their accountants, controllers, industrial engineers, and other staff members who pat them on *their* graying heads and tell them, "Not to worry—*our* reporting system is fine! Don't pay attention to that grumpy line supervisor or disgruntled hourly employee. They are chronic complainers."

We establish tracking and monitoring devices like standards—and we report on variances in part because we do not trust people to do their best. We want to know where to fix the blame. But because these evaluation tools are patently wrong—and our people know it—workers don't trust managers. Nor do workers trust management's staff, including our accountants. Workers certainly do not trust the information we provide them. The net result: We have thousands of drones busily producing reports "full of sound and fury—signifying nothing." Concomitantly, we have thousands of employees, hunkering down, spending their time and wasting their energy defending themselves.

This nonsense has to stop! We cannot comfort ourselves that accountants are unable to properly assess benefits with the fact that neither can they determine true costs. The damage is enormous. The problem urgently needs attention. But, before we blindfold them, stand them in front of a concrete wall, and grant them their last wishes, let's remember our original premise. They are generally nice, intelligent, well-meaning folk. Moreover, if we were to deal with them thus, then parity demands that we treat their bosses likewise. Notwithstanding that concrete walls are our present paradigms for handling poor performers, there is a better way that will produce a better world. Rather than "terminate" them, we should lead them to improve.

7
The Psychology of Controls

Two precepts. First, man can defeat any system man can devise. Second, the more controls you have, the less control you have.[1] Moreover, there is an inverse relationship between the number of controls and the trust in either the competence or the motives of the people in the organization.

If *control* means to direct or to lead—if it connotes the productive aspects of power and strength—it can contribute to the mission of the firm to design, produce, sell, distribute, and collect for a product or service that gets and keeps profitable customers. But control has a darker side—hindrance, constraint, repression, coercion—all subtractive, not additive, to the mission of the firm. True, the darker side of control is a mirror of the darker side of human nature. But this justification sometimes unchains the despot that is latent in all of us and allows a police state where a more open environment would better serve. In Freudian terms, the superego has not sublimated the id, it has transmogrified it.

The reasons for excessive control are complex. As has been suggested, some people crave petty power. Whether this is a result of sibling rivalry, anal retention, the Oedipus or Electra complex, is the subject of ponderous tomes filled with contradictory explanations. Suffice it to say, it is not the job of business leaders to diagnose the causes but rather to recognize the symptoms before placing someone of this persuasion in power.

Or, if a mistake in promotion has been made, to create an environment which mitigates the excesses! Or if that fails, then to remove the transgressor.

Excessive controls in organizations are sometimes the residue of past traumas. Say that the company responds to a poor financial performance with a new program for cost control. You are directed to produce head count reports as well as a dollar figure for direct and indirect labor. Moreover, overtime is to be cut by 40 percent and compliance is to be tracked—by cost center. In addition, a new mileage report is designed to report the percentage of time the salespeople are in their cars. Further, all travel expenses are to be reduced by 30 percent, and a report is devised to track the variances. Whether or not these are appropriate responses, do you think these reports are discontinued when business turns for the better? Rarely! Do you think they are reviewed during profitable periods? Perfunctorily, if at all. They persevere, however, wasting paper and chewing up time of those who prepare them as well as the users who have to make room for them on their desks or in their files.

Now let's propose an all-too-familiar scenario. Because of the press of other business, some of the control reports begin missing their deadlines. Let's say, also, that business takes another downturn. All of a sudden, "Where is that overtime report?" thunders out of the corner office. "I thought I told you I wanted it on my desk every Tuesday morning." From this day forward, that report and the others are firmly lodged. Neither castor oil nor gunpowder will dislodge them. Forget whether the overtime report is a useful tool, forget that producing these reports will replace other activities which might be more important. The reports will be prepared! On time! "Wait," you might protest. "The business turned down again. The reports were needed after all." Let's rephrase that. The information—not the reports—was needed.

If, however, the information is needed, we should ask next, "Who needs it?" If it is used by the corner office as a micromanagement tool, then more than overtime is out of control. More likely, the entire enterprise is out of control. If the people charged with managing direct labor and hundreds of other activities have such poor information—such a poor perception of the goals and business targets—then centralized micromanagement will suffer the same fate as the Supreme Soviet.

Some years ago, out of frustration, I attempted to centrally control direct labor hours in a supermarket chain. It was an unmitigated disaster. I did it because I had insufficient trust in the competence of the district and store managers. Worse, I put their integrity to the test, because in some instances their desire to run the store properly led them to do what was necessary, then to "cook" the weekly reports. Unwittingly, I required them to choose between lying to an ignorant boss and running the business properly. Fortunately, they chose to confront me with their dilemma. The ensuing discussions confirmed my suspicions but vindicated their actions. Many of them, indeed, needed training for better labor-hour scheduling techniques. They did not have the required skills—but the decree from "on high" worsened their plight. We began intensive training programs on the procedure for tying store labor schedules to forecasted sales—in units, not dollars. Then, we let the managers handle their own scheduling. Within a few months, store labor costs were in line.

Senior managers I have talked to mistakenly believe, as I did, that they are aware of the different drummers that different members of their organization are marching to; but almost invariably, these senior managers are the ones out of step. Even if they had come up through the ranks and had performed the tasks that they were now managing, their memories had dimmed and conditions had changed. In some instances, senior managers had forgotten the difficulty of managing disparate controls. Ask a plant manager to describe how he or she juggles the activities to meet the classic triumvirate targets—labor dollars, head count, and overtime. Ask the sales manager who has had to pull salespeople off the road because of a centrally ordained travel expense control.[2] Better still, ask these and other beleaguered managers to confess the shenanigans they have pulled in order to make the numbers.

In some instances, stringent controls are dictated by the task. As I suggested in an earlier book, the platoon under fire is ill served by laissez-faire.[3] It has almost no chance without discipline. The troops cannot sit by the side of the road, draw doodles in the sand, and debate whether to follow the leader or elect a new one. Businesses in crisis sometimes must resort to centralized, authoritarian control until the crisis passes. However, this verity is not eternal. Chances for survival are diminished unless the troops also have confidence in their leaders. Discipline without commitment might win skirmishes with ragamuffins but will not gain victory over those who possess both. Indeed, when the will to follow disappears, the leader nearly always is deposed. Even though the great despots of our century began with the enthusiastic support of their followers, these leaders were toppled or discredited as their ideas and actions tarnished. Hitler died in his bunker. Mussolini was hanged by his heels. Stalin has been disgraced, and Lenin's sculptors mourn the toppling of their once-towering icons.

Control is, then, a contradiction. In businesses as well as political systems, control is effective if those who are controlled concur that the controls are necessary and fair. Otherwise, people will disregard them, subvert them, or nibble them to death. If excessive controls are pervasive as well as onerous, people will organize to oppose them or will leave the enterprise, if not in body then—even worse—in spirit.

Stories are legion and are distressingly familiar. Most examples of waste cited in other chapters are results of onerous control systems. Expense account manipulations are legendary. Time sheet fairy tales and time clock partnerships are familiar artifices. Working by the book and rigidly adhering to job descriptions are costly charades. Circumventing head count controls with part-timers and consultants, not just fudging the numbers on financial reports but cooking the books—these are the sons and daughters of excessive controls.

As a manager of business turnarounds, I've heard it said that a business has cratered because its control system had broken down. Perhaps. But more often, it is because the control system has run amok. The princes who live higher up on the mountain have lost touch with the essential nature of their business. They have forgotten or never knew how hard it is sometimes to do the work. Unthinkingly, they have imposed systems, procedures, methods, policies, and practices which have little relationship to draining the swamp. They make their living by providing the alligators.

The irony is that these princes are subject to similar nonsense until they arrive at the very top of the mountain. So they participate in the same charade, only at higher altitudes. The implication is ineluctable: The higher the mountain, the more onerous the controls.

But does this mean that by nature humans abjure controls? Certainly not! Citizens of any community, business or political, will come together to enact laws and devise rules and regulations. To do otherwise is to support anarchy. Indeed, by harkening to our own darker side, we often prepare the way for despots by accepting more controls than we need. Erich Fromm, in his book *Escape from Freedom*, observed, as have other sociologists, that people sometimes shirk from responsibilities and from freedom and will choose to live under moderate conditions of tyranny.[4] Thoughtful leaders, like those who created our Bill of Rights, have understood this tendency and have provided alternatives that are designed to save us from ourselves.

How then, you might ask, can I suggest that people are oppressed by controls when at the same time they embrace them? The answer is in the excesses: excesses in scope and rigidity. When people find themselves trammeled at every turn by rules and regulations, and when they find that the rules and regulations so tightly constrain that their growth is stunted and their judgment is excluded, they will chafe, they will become troublemakers, or they will find ways to dismantle the system. None of these activities are what the founders or shareholders had in mind when they created or financed the enterprise.

Controls in organizations are necessary, certainly! Excessive controls are destructive. Here is one way to determine which are necessary and which are not. First, and always, the decision should be made in the context of a clear understanding of the aim, mission, goals, and objectives of the organization and its units. In that context, the following questions should be asked:

What controls are absolutely necessary to achieve our aim?

Where should these controls be located?

How should they be monitored?

Generally, controls that survive the first question will address product and corporate integrity. They will deal with the major attributes of quality, how people in the organization are treated, how customers and suppliers will be treated. Of course, they will deal with the prevention of dishonest and illegal practices.

Once the necessary controls are identified, locating them will be relatively easy. They should be located closest to those doing the work.

As always, authority can be assigned. Responsibility remains at the top. In that context, a monitoring system will need to be determined. Just as some products require final inspection, those issues which address the life or death of an enterprise should also have the oversight of senior managers. The method and frequency will be determined by degree of trust and the importance of the control. Those who are interested in a methodology for removing excessive measurements and controls should review Appendix C—"Conducting the Measurement and Control Audit."

PART 2

Trust and Competence

If everyone knew what to do, how, when, and where to do it, what would the organization structure look like?

The implicit promise of this utopia might be unachievable, but the quest will be profitable. However, the quest for competence as a concept alone is not enough. Socrates refused to equate knowledge with virtue. Competence without morality is dangerous. Competence without aim, vision, mission, values, goals, and objectives is meaningless. Moreover, competence is more than education and training programs. It is more than hiring and promotion policies. It is more than information, tools, and technology, important as they are. Competence is not the exclusive preserve of the human resources department; it is everybody's business—a corporate state of mind—as natural as breathing.

Competence will be found where managers and employees are, daily, learning from one another; where they are learning from customers, suppliers, and competitors; where information exchange is easy and open—up, down, across, inside, and outside the organization; where managers and employees are open to new theory, new applications, new methods, procedures, and policies.

Moreover, competence cannot be defined in terms of costs or benefits. Only a few of the costs are measurable. The benefits cannot be measured but they can be understood. One can understand, but how can one measure the value of a loyal customer base rather than one that is restless and opportunistic? How would one measure the loss and benefits from disgruntled customers who tell others about their unhappiness?

But competence is understood when encountered—when a phone call is answered by someone who is knowledgeable, cheerful, and helpful; when a query or complaint is handled quickly and satisfactorily without "I'll put you on hold; my department doesn't handle that." Competence is reflected when the invoices are always understandable and correct, when the product or service not only meets but exceeds expectations, when the packaging is right and the delivery is on time.

The costs are embedded in every action, the benefits in every outcome. The true measure is not how much, but how. Certainly, the costs should be tailored to fit the resources, but the best part of competence is free. It begins and ends with knowledgeable, consistently improving individuals working to the same end, using interactive management processes in an open, trusting environment and a permeable organization structure.

8

The Permeable Organization Structure

When we do not trust the competence of people, we supervise them. Traditional organization hierarchies suggest cascading rungs of police and inspectors. When people's jobs occur in different functions, we coordinate them. Narrowly defined functional responsibilities sometimes create barriers behind which people can hide while shifting blame. When the jobs seem too big, we break them into smaller pieces, and then we coordinate them. These presumptions of incompetence are the roots of towering hierarchy, functional isolationism, and overspecialization. Unfortunately, the presumptions of incompetence are sometimes correct. The world has plenty of well-meaning, bright, and incompetent people. There are also those who are not so well-meaning or bright. The answer to this problem only rarely is to add structure or process controls. Instead, we should address directly the shortcomings of individuals, we should open up our business processes and remove excessive communication and coordination requirements of the organization functions and hierarchy. In practice, it is futile to address these three issues separately, but for purposes of discussion we will look at them one at a time. In this chapter we will focus on the structure and its two major elements: functions and hierarchy.[1]

Functions and hierarchy are the X and Y axes of our organization charts. Complexity is directly related to the length of these axes, and trust is usually inversely related. As we have seen, management processes for the purpose of integrating activities that have been balkanized by the structure are only partially successful. To breach the boundaries of functions and hierarchies, we invented matrix structures, which, unfortunately, spawn even more interstices where suspicion can be harbored. In creative desperation, we have invented organization charts using concentric circles, squares, rectangles, and inverted pyramids. If we believe in the theory of holes, however, we should stop inventing. Creating new structures and more processes without addressing causes will not solve our problems. Any system devised by man can be defeated by man. Unless the humans in the system believe it is fair and unless they believe in the aim or mission of the enterprise, the search for the perfect organization structure or system will meet the fate of Sisyphus. But if the structure and its processes are user-friendly, they will be cordially embraced. We shall propose some structural improvements. First some theory, then some history which might enhance our understanding of the need for improvement.

Diseconomies of Scope, Scale, and Size

Time and time again we have found that theoretical economies of scale and scope are overwhelmed by the cost of coordination, integration, and supervision. If complexity is directly correlated to the length of the axes representing hierarchical function and if the coordination of complex activities raises costs, the straightforward approach is to reduce the length of the axes: Cut layers to eliminate unnecessary supervision and combine functions to deal with overspecialization.

Scope

In the 1940s, Erich Fromm wrote about the cobbler who built a pair of shoes from lasts to laces. He then sold them to a neighbor, and watched out his window as the neighbor wore down the heels, then the soles. The cobbler could fairly well predict when this customer would return for repairs. He had a close relationship with his product and his customer. His business practices were straightforward. He put his receipts in his pocket. From that, he paid for more leather and nails, bought a new hammer and knife, bought his food, paid for his housing, and, with luck, put a little away.

We have just described the management and supervision of design, purchasing, manufacturing, marketing, sales, customer service, human relations, MIS, accounting, and finance. And the cobbler didn't even have an MBA.

Then came Henry Ford and many others who were following theory first proposed by Plato, developed further by Adam Smith in his famous pin factory, and by Charles Babbage. These people said that greater efficiency could be achieved by breaking the job into parts—assigning one person to cut the leather, another to cut the soles, another to cut the heels, another to nail the heels and then another to nail the soles, another to collect the money, and so on. Along the way, we invented machines which could do the jobs even faster. People still would be required to run the machines—but we would need fewer of them. As history shows, Henry Ford was right. Specialists dramatically reduced direct costs. Yes, the savings were offset somewhat by the cost of coordination, supervision, and the maintenance of the machines. Furthermore, there were the added capital costs of factories and machinery—but even then, we could made shoes cheaper. By hiring specialists in design, we could make the shoes more comfortable and more handsome or attractive. We hired scientists and technicians to develop new and better materials which not only improved appearance and durability but permitted new manufacturing techniques which cut costs even more. Wonderful! But, as we broke the job into more and more tasks, we needed more and more people for supervision. Gradually, supervision, not shoemaking, became the work of this new cadre. The closer these supervisors came to the sources of power, the more influence they gained. Then, as rewards systems were developed which paid people according to their levels in the hierarchy, supervisors were added to supervise supervisors, and on and on. But even then we did not worry. We in the United States had a head start on the rest of the world. Our shoes, automobiles, and other goods were far better and less expensive.

Scale

So we got bigger! Profits and external sources of capital permitted us to build not one but dozens of factories whose activities were coordinated by more supervision, corporate specialists in production, marketing, and the other functions. We found sources of public capital which let us hire professional managers who had no direct financial stake and who often came from the supervisory ranks. Many of these felt that their jobs were to supervise the system, not to improve it. Nevertheless profits continued to grow even as we added more supervisors and more people to measure the work, to control the money, and to distribute the information needed.

But Erich Fromm was not writing only about production economics. He was writing about alienation of workers from their work, their product, their customer. The people who watched over the machine which drove the short nails may not have known what the finished shoe would look like. Certainly, they would not know the wearer of the shoes. Even the supervisor who watched over the persons who watched the machines which drove the short and the long nails had no real knowledge of end use. Or the supervisor who supervised all the nails or the "really big boss" who supervised both nails and stitching may not have known. These supervisors and their colleagues produced reports. Numbers nailed, numbers stitched, percentage scrap, percentage rejects, machine utilization, cost per unit nailed, cost per unit stitched, cost per unit nailed and stitched, attendance, absenteeism, units per man hour. Our management cadre was producing numbers, not shoes.

Industrial engineers came along and established standards. Now the supervisor was measured on variance from standard. More importantly, this supervisor's numbers and variances were compared to other supervisors in the plant—and supervisors in other plants. Bonuses and promotions depended on supervisor's ranking with others. To the extent that those who reported to the supervisor failed to produce the desired numbers, they became the enemy. Now there were adversaries all around—up, down, and across. Trust disappeared.

In this environment workers became increasingly alienated. They organized to bargain collectively for wages and work rules. "No, the worker should not nail 1200 nails per hour—only 700. And the company cannot move the worker to the stitching machine without a pay premium." To supervise this system, a parallel system of "management" was added: shop stewards, plant stewards, managers of local unions, along with their administrators, accountants, and finance specialists. Some of the money paid to them was used for strike benefits and to organize other plants or other industries. Some of the money was used for lobbying, some was used for managing the union superstructure. Although it may have appeared that these activities were paid for by the worker, it all went back into the cost of the shoes. Still, all was fine. American manufacturing continued to prosper and grow.

But we were living on borrowed time. During the 1960s and early 1970s, U.S. companies became aware of more and more shoes and other goods from overseas. Their quality and design were not so bad and were getting better. Prices were lower. "It's the cheap labor," we told ourselves. To an extent we were right, particularly in regard to high labor content and low valued-added products. Not to worry. We'll either shift our production to low-wage countries or in some cases we will abandon that line of work. But as the companies in low-wage countries made money, they were able to purchase the same machinery we were using. Now they had both state-of-the-art machinery and low labor costs. Furthermore their capital costs often were lower, making their machines much less expensive. "Unfair," we said. "We have to level the playing field." "Quotas and tariffs are needed." "The dollar is too dear." Then, when the Japanese and West German wage cost reached parity with ours, we justified our positions with the disparities in currency values and capital costs. Then we found other excuses: The competitors had morning calisthenics, company songs, government assistance, a culture which produced a docile labor force and a supervisory cadre who were willing to work 14 hours a day. But we still needed to explain away the increasing technical competence and innovative ability of our adversaries. So, in the 1980s we consoled ourselves with data that showed the United States was in the lead in technological break-throughs. That helped us bear the realization that even though we invented the microwave oven and VCR, none were manu-factured here. Radios and dozens of other transistor-based products were no longer manufactured here either. Only one television manufacturer remained. Again, we comforted our-selves with the explanation that our off-shore competitors were good copiers, good adaptors. "We'll ultimately win with break-through technology."

It wasn't until the late 1980s that serious doubts were enter-tained about the validity of our excuses. Dr. W. Edwards Deming had been warning us for decades, but we had ignored him. Now, as we studied our successful competitors, we found that in addition to company songs and a supportive government, their system of management was more effective and more efficient: fewer organizational layers by far; less supervision because they trained their workers to do much of their inspection; less specialization because their workers were cross-trained and their work rules permitted employees to per-form many tasks, as needed; fewer maintenance workers, because the shop floor worker was trained and permitted by work rules to perform maintenance tasks. And we found a lot more trust. We found a management group that was willing to listen and to learn from the people doing the work—not just the engineers. Hence we found quality circles which were worker driven, not management driven. We found also that the engi-neers were cross-trained. Newly graduated engineers were sent out on marketing and sales jobs in order to better understand the customers. By the time someone became a senior manager, she or he had held several functional positions. All the forego-ing are examples of greater organizational competence made possible in part by a permeable organization structure that allowed easy access across functions and more effective interac-tion in a shorter chain of command.

Size

Back to Erich Fromm's cobbler. Is big always bad? Was Schumacher right: "Small is beautiful"?[2] Big is bad to the extent that control and coordination stifle creative participation and otherwise alienate managers and employees. These corrosive conditions, however, exist in smaller organizations. In that context, big is not bad perforce. Indeed, big is a necessity in some industries if companies are to successfully compete—especially if they compete globally. But if big becomes a state of mind which glorifies size rather than agility, and if big thoughtlessly encourages the growth of the hierarchy and the proliferation of functions, then it needs to be cut down to size. Jack Welch has said that he wants General Electric to be run like a $70 billion popcorn stand. The company's actions sometimes belie his words, but Welch's intention is clear: He wants to eliminate the waste created by bureaucracy and to instill the value of speed, simplicity, and self-confidence.

My own belief is that organizations tend to excessive size—size not measured by dollars but by the number, complexity, and inefficiency of information carriers: people, structure, and processes.[3] The earlier discussion suggested one way of reducing size by shortening the hierarchy and combining the functions. Hierarchies and functions breed mistrust. Mistrust breeds hierarchies and functions. The common denominator is mistrust. Until it is eliminated, or at least ameliorated, no meaningful change in structure or process will be possible.

The Hierarchy

The organizational hierarchy serves best which trains its people, then integrates and coordinates their activities. Its antithesis is command and control—inspector, police, sometimes mule driver. The assumption driving this obsolete model is that the bosses know how to do jobs better than the people who are doing the work, that people dislike their jobs, that they will not make their quotas unless driven or paid by the piece, that to meet numerical quotas they will knowingly turn out substandard work. These expectations are self-fulfilling:

"People are not trustworthy!" Sure enough, they're not. Ergo, "The system works!"

Managing the hierarchy also drives assumptions about span of control, an almost casually used descriptor freighted with meaning. It calls to mind another system devoid of trust—prison guards and prison work groups. Perhaps a farfetched analogy, but close enough to make the point.

Assume that one prison guard can handle 5 or 6, but not 100, inmates. Unless, of course, the guard puts them in chains! That's it! A breakthrough in management theory borrowed from society's growth industry.

The short span of control, in turn, dictates the number of guards as well as the number of guard supervisors. Let's call the guards "line supervisors" and their supervisors "section heads." With a span of control of 5 inmates, 20 line supervisors and 4 section heads will be needed for each 100 prisoners. If the prison has 1000 inmates, then 200 line supervisors will be needed who, in turn, are supervised by 40 section heads who require 8 group heads who then require 2 area heads, who in turn report to an executive vice president in charge of work gangs. We have 251 people in "management" not counting the warden—a ratio not of 1 to 5—but now 1 to 4. This is the logical outcome of the pyramid effect—and we now have six layers between the warden and the worker. If our span of control were 10 we would need about half as many managers—111.

The foregoing is not to suggest fewer prison guards. One-on-one may be more appropriate in some prisons. But it is anathema in today's business world. The command-and-control model with short spans of control creates enormous losses: direct losses measured by excessive management costs and indirect losses measured by degradation of information as it travels up and down the golden staircase. These losses, although great, pale in comparison to costs associated with the workers' loss of motivation to excel in their jobs as defined—or to redefine and improve methods of accomplishing their tasks. Furthermore, the costs increase geometrically as the workers move up the skills ladder or management hierarchy. Inappropriate as the control hierarchy may be for low-skill or repetitive tasks, it is folly when used with information and knowledge workers, middle managers, and remote units such as sales offices and service centers.

The Functions

If my MBA candidates ask, "Is this a finance or a marketing problem?" my answer is "Yes." Very few business problems can be isolated. As everyone knows, a successful marketing program requires financial support—but such a program also requires good manufacturing and distribution. Before that, it requires good design and purchasing. Order entry and billing systems are necessary to support the sale. Accounting is needed to keep track of the cash and profits and losses. Banks and other financial sources are needed, as are suppliers and customers. Nothing new here. The word *team* is one of the most popular words in business. I've noticed, however, that its greatest use is by those on the higher rungs of the ladder—and is usually preceded by the pronoun *my*. Down the ladder, one hears the word *team* rarely. Even more rarely is it preceded by the word *our*. Sometimes the word is *their*.

In one instance that I observed, the marketing department drew up concepts for a new product and then handed it over to the design engineers. Almost a year went by before the purchasing agent was asked whether he could purchase the material in sufficient quantities at the right price. Manufacturing was never asked whether they could build it—never mind whether they could build it on time or on budget. The sales department was not consulted. Long after the product failed and a new project was under way, I asked the marketing vice president if the salespeople had been consulted this time. When he responded "Yes," I asked what their responses had been. He replied, "We don't really listen to them. They're just salesmen. And they don't know our problems, so we just punch their tickets." The permeable structure, the hallmark of competent organizations, was the victim of functional isolationism. The product and the company suffered. The development cycle was twice as long as it should have been, and, chances are, the new product will fail also.

In another instance, marketing and sales vice presidents pre-pared their business plans without ever talking to their manu-facturing and distribution counterparts. Yes, they were given 2 or 3 pages of economic assumptions and a hurriedly concocted strategic statement. The heroic assumption was that the division staff would coordinate the various functional plans, then referee the fight for resources. Open, interactive communication, again, was absent. Any competence the organization had possessed was bottled up in the functions and was therefore limited. It would have expanded geometrically had information been shared across functions.

Another especially poignant example: A small manufacturing company on the verge of bankruptcy was holding a last desper-ate meeting of its senior managers. Suppliers had cut them off, so the manufacturing plant was about to shut down. During the meeting, the marketing vice president, who had never been in the plant and had never met the manufacturing vice president, mentioned a product for which he had a large order but which was not in the current catalog. The manufacturing vice presi-dent perked up and said, "I can build that. We have a ware-house full of material for that product." Unfortunately, it was too late for this coordination to help. The company did not sur-vive. Perhaps the lost sale would not have made the difference, but the company will never know.

Overspecialization

Overspecialization is in part due to the complexity of today's business world. Specialists are increasingly necessary. The sophisticated tools used by marketing research require well-trained theorists and practitioners. Metals and plastics techni-cians can spend their lifetimes learning. A specialist's full atten-tion is required to manage swaps or coordinate international currencies. Well-trained technicians are required for computer-managed decision support systems. But this call for excellence in their specialties does not mean that any of them can afford to live in splendid isolation. The question which naturally follows is how they will find the time to interact productively if so much time is required to discharge their daily responsibilities while maintaining competence in their special fields. The answer is essentially the same as it was for the New England supermarket personnel, who were spending one-half of their time in the paper chase—documenting activities for the benefit of headquarters personnel. We have to eliminate the bureaucratic nonsense that is spawned by the command-and-control hierarchy and by functional isolationism.

Too many specialists and scientists I have talked to also are covered up with "administrivia." Some of them go along with the system—at great loss to themselves and to the organization. Others rebel—refuse to comply—thus earning their stripes as eccentrics or troublemakers. Some of the rebels are so good at their work that the organization accommodates them. Other rebels turn sour—more reclusive—until the organization gives up—decides to fence them off or asks them to leave.

Universities are not immune to overspecialization. Business researchers dig deeper and narrower holes. Refereed journals are often incomprehensible except to the referees. The analytical models offered in these journals may be technically correct as defined but often lack critically important input from different disciplines which would drastically alter the outcomes. Recently I read an article based on a mathematical model of a manufacturing process. It was written by three respected academicians, who were using elegant math, and it was published in a respected academic journal. The model had holes in it big enough to drive a forklift through. Had the good professors consulted their colleagues in manufacturing and production, or had they consulted with a practitioner, they could have saved energy, reputation, ink, two or three trees, and perhaps a spotted owl. Overspecialization and insufficient interaction did them in.

Although the tendency in business and academe has been toward greater specialization, many examples from science and business demonstrate that cross-fertilization is and has been alive and well. The Manhattan Project, which developed the atomic bomb, would not have been successful if the scientists from different fields had not daily worked together in that small building underneath the football stadium.

Much of the research on diseases of the retina is now center-
ing on nutrition. The literature on innovation has many examples on the power of external stimuli. Brewster Ghiselin's book,
The Creative Process, reported conversations with the great math-
ematician Henri Poincaré who reported that external stimuli
outside his own field had been prompters of his breakthrough
insights.[4] Steven Jay Gould is a specialist in evolution, a generalist as well as a scientist, and at least a borderline renaissance
man. Cross-fertilization of his wide range of interests is apparent in his rich offerings.

On the shop floor and in administrative work, the problems
of overspecialization are addressed by cross-training. Indeed, if
the job is defined broadly enough, it is not cross-training but
training for a bigger job. Nothing really new here on the manufacturing scene. Although many companies still hew to the traditional production line orientation, cellular manufacturing and
other processes have been addressing overspecialization for
years. Toyota addresses this issue directly in its employee manual. For instance, the manual states that in Japan there is usually
no job description for an employee. However, the responsibility
of the group or section is clearly defined. The manual goes on to
say that the employee is expected to be qualified to handle several jobs within his or her group. Moreover, Toyota has, as do
many Japanese companies, large-scale staff reassignments in
February or March. The company follows this practice not only
to develop generalists but also to develop a large circle of
acquaintances in the organization, which they go on to say is
one of the greatest assets of Japanese workers and managers.

The move away from overspecialization has not progressed as
far in administrative work as it has in manufacturing and production; however, there are notable examples, particularly in
self-supervised accounts payable groups. My colleague E. Kirby
Warren reports on an insurance company which experimented
with a self-supervised accounts payable section that was one-
half the size of the other sections yet produced 40 percent more
work, essentially error-free. I had similar success 20 years ago
with a self-supervised group at a supermarket company. Mike
Hammer reported in his now-famous *Harvard Business Review*
article on reengineering about an insurance company which

reduced from 13 to 1 the number of people required to approve new insurance policies. Turnaround time was reduced from 5 to 25 days down to 2 to 5 days—some in as little as four hours, and the work force was substantially reduced.[5]

The Quest for Permeability—Horizontal versus Vertical

Business books and journals regularly report examples of companies that are breaking down the barriers in the chain of command and between functions. General Electric's quest for the boundaryless organization has received much attention. Asea Brown Boveri has dealt similarly with the chain of command by abolishing it—with the exception of two layers. Tom Peters suggests the RIP organization process—rip it up and start all over again.[6] Mike Hammer has said, "Obliterate, not automate."[7] I have said for years that we should throw away most of the business textbooks on organization, shred organization charts, and burn the policy manuals. We can preserve institutional learning and exercise necessary control through interactive processes, and we can eliminate waste and complexity if we shift our thinking about business from vertical to horizontal. But all of us are latecomers to this insight. W. Edwards Deming, in 1950, suggested the move toward horizontal organizations when he developed the organizational flow diagram that showed the interdependence of suppliers, producers, and customers. Recently, Dr. Nida Backaitis, Dr. Deming's associate, has suggested that the famous Deming model is also an organization chart. His model not only shows reporting relationships—where the person fits in the process—but it helps people to understand what their jobs are. A traditional pyramid shows only who reports to whom. Moreover, two of the groups that are central to the process—suppliers and customers—are conspicuously absent from the traditional vertical chart.

Although I believe that the structure of very few enterprises will look vertical in the years to come, it will not be necessary for all businesses to immediately destroy their present structure in order to achieve greater permeability. Task forces and other temporary structural mechanisms that have been so well reported will help to create horizontal permeability. Business processes described in the next chapter will also loosen the bonds of restrictive structure, but all these changes will ultimately be just cosmetic—permeability will not be achieved—if business is conducted in a climate of mistrust, if people, activities, and functions are evaluated narrowly, with the supposition that they can act independently of each other. Competence also is crucial to permeability, as is appreciation for a system, trustworthy information, and high integrity. The absence of these will sooner or later warp any changes back into the fortress structure and will foster the defensive processes that foster so much complexity and waste.

Dealing with the five causes of mistrust, important as they are for traditional structures, will be even more important to the new horizontal structures. A task force whose members do not trust the motives or competence of one another will be worse than no task force at all—better to revert to the traditional control hierarchy than to run the risk that the task force will self-destruct. But sometimes there can be a silver lining to the stresses found in these task forces. The stresses not only will highlight the need for trust, they should also dramatize the need and pave the way for changes required for improving trust.

Vertical to Horizontal

Let's look now at some of the outcomes of horizontal thinking.

Task forces have been used for years. They can serve as a model for other changes. They can exist for one day or for a year or more. Task forces can be particularly useful to the company that has not yet used horizontal structures. Caution: Do not overuse. A seminar participant who had formerly worked with a large personal computer company told me that at one time he was on 32 task forces, yet continued to have functional responsibility. Another caution: If functions still hold the power in the reward system, the person assigned to task forces will quite correctly be concerned about evaluation of her or his work. A very competent in-house lawyer who was assigned to spend half of his time on an industry task force received a mediocre rating at his annual review time. He was livid. "How do they know what I have been doing?"

Teams are usually longer-lived than task forces. They can be used for special projects—new product development or introductions—or can be organized more or less permanently around product teams, where several people from various functions work together only on one product or one product group.

The General Motors light truck plant in Shreveport is organized around the team concept, and it regularly posts the greatest productivity of any of the General Motors plants, including the famed Nummi plant, the GM-Toyota joint venture modeled on Japanese management methods.

Process teams can be, for example, people from various functions working on an expanded concept of customer service, which might include order entry, distribution interface, product or service complaints, billing adjustments, special pricing, etc. In some instances, people on these teams can hold multiple assignments; however, joining and rejoining can create information lag, thereby adding to the complexity and subtracting from the consistency of the effort.

Customer teams can be project assignments or relatively permanent assignments to an important customer or to a specific customer group. Companies that serve Wal-Mart and other power retailers often have permanent teams based at or near customer headquarters. Technology-based companies use customer teams for major installation projects. Consulting and other knowledge-based companies have been using the customer team model for years.

Some precautions are in order here. Changing from a vertical to a horizontal structure through use of teams can look great on paper, but the change does not happen automatically. New communication channels must be opened. Information systems need to be reconfigured. If, for instance, a product team is responsible for customer interface, how are billing problems to be resolved? If the expanded customer service team has all the contacts with the customers, where will pricing information be located, what pricing authority will repose in customer service, how will the salespeople be kept in the loop? Similar issues need to be resolved with customer teams. For instance, what will be the team's relationship to the company's product managers? How will scheduling conflicts in manufacturing and distribution be resolved?

These problems are obviously not insurmountable, but they need to be addressed if the new horizontal structure is to be successful. In some respects, the solution might be described as an iteration of the matrix structure. I am not suggesting here that a matrix structure be adopted, because the term *matrix* is limited and the matrix has been tarnished by its many failures. But the matrix structure itself might not have been the problem. The problem could have been in the evaluation system—evaluations not only of the employee who worked for two bosses but between the two bosses themselves in their struggle for recognition and power. The compensation system that was proposed in Chapter 5 will ameliorate the stress but will not remove it completely. Even if the new structure were to have some aspects of the matrix organization, it should not slavishly imitate any other model but should be tailored to fit the requirements of the situation. Tom Peters's "clean sheet of paper" may be the best way to proceed. And creation of the design that goes on that paper should not be delegated to a consultant or a human resources department. They can provide guidance, certainly, but if operating managers and information sources are not actively involved, the design will not only suffer the NIH (not invented here) problem, but much more importantly, it might not meet the broad requirements and certainly not the nuances of the firm's strategy and its operations.

One last admonition: Teams and task forces can look good conceptually but will not be effective over time if they do not address the career needs of their members. If people are removed from home base where their performance is assessed, where job assignments are made, and where pay and promotion decisions are determined, task forces and teams will not be successful in the traditional organization. They of course have been successful for years in more informal organizations like consulting firms and high-technology organizations. For permeability to improve in the traditional organization, functions must lose some of their power—perhaps better said: They should share their power.

Town meetings, introduced by General Electric, are now being used in various forms by other firms. They usually bring together suppliers, customers, and people in the company—across functions and up and down the hierarchy—to work on a common problem. Two of the requirements for success are: The problem must be well defined and not too broadly stated; and data about the problem should be gathered, codified, and in some instances analyzed and distributed to the participants prior to the meeting. Without these two requirements, the town meeting could degenerate into an expensive bull session. Companies sometimes begin with big meetings with 60 to 80 people, who are assigned to groups that will specialize in various aspects of the problem, then come together at the end of the process to make their recommendations. These big meetings are useful for kicking off the process, but over time are too cumbersome and expensive. They serve their purpose if they break down organizational barriers and serve as a model for smaller problem-solving groups. As one GE work-out consultant said, "They should become 'natural acts in natural places.'"

Prahalad and Hamel report on another structural change that promotes permeability among *core competencies*.[8] Rather than organize by customer project, product, or the more traditionally organized functional strategic business unit (SBU) with its implicit profit responsibilities, Canon and NEC have tailored their organizations around the core competencies. This organizational form, which seems best suited for technology companies, fosters cross-fertilization among scientists and technicians who, otherwise, would be isolated—working in their own areas of specialization. Freed from the constraints of traditional structure, companies that organize around core competencies seem to develop better products, faster and less expensively.

Building on Prahalad and Hamel's work, George Stalk, Philip Evans, and Lawrence Shulman observe that some companies are organized around *core capabilities*.[9] Their centerpiece example is Wal-Mart, which has identified logistics and communications as those most critical to its success. Wal-Mart's communication system directs product flow, and the logistics system gets product to the stores on time. Suppliers are integral to the information systems, which are incredibly permeable. Information exchange is quick and comprehensive. But suppliers must similarly have permeability that permits information exchange and the capability to move quickly, or they will not be suppliers for very long. One of the more dramatic examples of structural permeability at Wal-Mart is the interaction of buying, merchandising, and store operations. Traditionally, buying and/or merchandising is a separate and distinct function from store operations. Not at Wal-Mart.

I am a member of the board of directors at two retailing firms—one, a women's fashion retailer, and another, a large general merchandise retailer. I can attest to the wars and the attendant communication lapses that exist because merchandising and operations are separate, distinct, and evaluated as if they were independent entities. And in the food retailing operation that I led, I noted that when the vice president of merchandising wished to infuriate his counterpart in operations, he would say, "I am the architect and engineer—you're just the contractor." In most instances that I have observed, merchant/buyer intransigence is the primary culprit in losses from this organization failure. Intransigence is responsible not just because of the administrative waste and complexity created, but also because merchandisers do not properly read the customer, or store's ability to translate the merchandising concepts to the customer.

Wal-Mart has ended the war, first by removing much of the power from headquarters buyers and second by blurring the distinction between merchandising and operations. Most merchandising decisions at Wal-Mart are made by operations people who are in the stores. Then the permeability among the functions—buying, merchandising, operations, and distribution—is dramatized by Wal-Mart's famed Saturday morning meetings, with as many as 500 people in attendance, where information is shared, where decisions are made, and where plans are formed on the spot for next week's activities. Wal-Mart could not exist with the traditional command-and-control hierarchy and functional isolationism. Structural permeability is one of its greatest assets.

Nordstrom Department Stores has now moved much of the buying responsibility to the stores. This move has been costly; it creates havoc when hordes of Nordstrom buyers from all over the country descend on the market at the same time—but Nordstrom keeps getting it right. The customer prevails over organizational niceties. The extra cost is well worth it.

Colocation it the new organizational buzzword that reflects the importance of geography in business operations. When managers suggest that colocation creates confusion and/or unacceptable noise levels, I tell them about reorganization task forces with which I have worked. We usually commandeer a shabby office somewhere, bring in some tables and folding chairs, install a few phones, and "We're in business." If the person we want to talk to is across the room, we can walk to her or his desk. More often than not, we just sing out our questions and responses. It doesn't seem to bother the others. Indeed, it may broadcast information that will be valuable to them also.

Manufacturing companies are now locating design engineers on the plant floor—to the initial discomfort of the design engineers. But in most cases, they ultimately have become enthusiastic about the change. Their output improves and they develop a closer relationship to the end product.

I recently visited a small manufacturing operation—about $60 million in revenues—that had replaced its MRP II system and several employees by colocating the plant scheduler and the purchasing director. They were within speaking distance of each other. Moreover, they were within 50 feet of the plant's operations manager. Furthermore, the company had verified its commitment to horizontal thinking in its relationship with suppliers. All materials were sole-sourced. The suppliers had become a seamless adjunct to the team. Daily inventories were conducted—visually—by the purchasing manager, who reported enthusiastically that not only was raw in process (RIP) inventory held to a very few days, but that since the inception of the new procedures and the colocation with the plant scheduler, no plant shutdowns or scheduling problems had occurred.

Zytec locates its purchasing managers with its design engineers. No more "throwing the specs over the wall" to the purchasing manager with the instructions, "Go get some quotes." Now the purchasing manager at Zytec takes a profession interest in searching out new and better materials and better ways of using them.

Examples are legion. But any changes in one component of an extant system will trigger changes in the system. So the information flows and management processes need to reflect these organizational changes. And of course colocation cannot be taken to absurd lengths. During a recent planning meeting, one executive in mock disgust cautioned, "If colocation picks up much more momentum around here, we'll have to rent the Superdome and some folding chairs." This caution notwithstanding, companies in their quest for structural permeability are using colocation as one of their organizational tools.

Small is beautiful. Task forces or teams should be small enough so that each member can know the other and can know what work the others are doing. The team should be small enough that all communication is oral and that competence is readily observable. Creation of a number of small work units will of course create its own problems of coordination. Each firm should develop the communication system that best suits its needs. But the effort will be richly rewarded by the fact that communication is now focused on the customer, the product, or the process—not functions or the chain of command.

Although specialists are always needed, the quest for permeability implies that the specialists acquire more general knowledge of how their activities can more effectively contribute to the whole—and in some instances, the specialists should be allowed the fun of playing the generalist role.

Finally, everyone needs to be *customer-focused*. Whether in the traditional vertical structure or in the horizontally focused structure, greater permeability will be achieved if each person can answer affirmatively the following: Am I helping to design, produce, sell, distribute, and collect for a product or service whose goal is to get and keep profitable customers?

9
Interactive Processes

If functions and hierarchies are the structure of an organization, processes are the systems which give it life. They provide direction through planning and budgeting, they provide controls through financial and operational reviews, they provide feedback through information and reports, and they provide coordination through meetings, memos, and other communication tools. Here we will examine a few of these processes to learn not only why they so often go awry but also how we can improve them.

Budgets and Business Plans

One of our most damaging time wasters is the preparation of the annual operating budget. If Leonard Bernstein were still alive, I would ask him to write a ballet about budgeting—the steps are predictable if not beautiful, and the music would sound more like the Grateful Dead than Tchaikovsky.

Typically, the budget–business planning process begins in July or August—earlier in some firms. Senior management personnel issue financial guidelines—for instance, 15 percent growth and 20 percent return on assets employed. Although not intended to do so, these guidelines sometimes influence the operations for many of the smaller budgeting units, whether or not the 15-20 rule applies. Some are support functions and should not be judged financially. Other units may add strategic value to the product portfolio. The attempt to conform them to the 15-20 rule can lead to pricing mistakes or to resource starving. In other instances, managers make strategic allowances for the units under their purview, but when their departmental or divisional budget is rolled up, it must meet the 15-20 guidelines. Some companies use the same guidelines year after year with the justification that the stock market rewards consistency. Only a few companies are able to pull this off over time. Other companies pay a terrible price if they have, over time, made short-term decisions that were detrimental to the long-term health of the firm. For example, a well-known global company uses similar guidelines. According to some of this company's executives, the worldwide price inflation of the products they sell was in 1992 between 1 and 2 percent. The rest of the growth—to meet the 15-20 guideline—would have to come from new products or from incremental market share. But increased market share will not come from the tooth fairy. Sometimes sheer genius will do it. More often, however, increased market share requires new distribution or marketing expenses. Caught in a double bind of current soft sales and the profitability target, managers are reluctant to take the marketing expenditure risk. New products present a similar conundrum. New products require investment, only some of which can be capitalized. New products introduced in an unfriendly economic environment carry a lot of risk. The costs generally are known. The revenues are not. Because the risk is high, product portfolio decisions that are important to the company's market position are often postponed.

In both scenarios, the managers are facing the realization that they cannot meet both the growth and the profitability guidelines. So they devise various survival strategies. Too often, these strategies are for their *personal* survival, not the firm's. One of these is "Damn the torpedoes and full speed ahead. Budget for the sales increase and the profits, then pray for a miracle." Happily, for budgeting purposes, the sales increase pulls up the profit number on the budget. This survival strategy buys managers some time—say, until the beginning of the third quarter when the managers now have no choice but to admit that their budget is in trouble. They can appear heroic by slashing costs that had been ramped up by the aggressive sales target. But the earlier ramping up requires Draconian ramping down—the type of downsizing that destroys trust as well as future prospects of the business. Another ploy is to borrow sales from the next quarter or the following year. Let's say, though, that stark reality finally intervenes. It becomes clear that they cannot make the numbers. If the entire firm is in the same shape, they can hide along with their peers under the shroud of a lousy economy. Nevertheless, the company pays the piper. The aggressive revenue projection has also ramped up inventory levels, which almost always requires that sooner or later the inventory be discounted or reserved because of obsolescence. Happily for the budgeteers with short-term views, decisions to add to reserves are not always made during the present budget year. The budgeteers comfort themselves with the thought, "We'll cover this up when times are better."

Another strategy is to budget for lower sales and to begin to cut costs. Of the two, this strategy is directionally the best, but the execution is usually flawed. The budget timetable prevents managers from making process changes which reduce costs through elimination of complexity and waste. Instead, they hurriedly cut costs that might be important to the long-term health of the firm. Again, the negative effects of the cost-cutting strategy are usually not immediately apparent. The advertising and marketing cuts might create risks for future market position. Moreover, productive people who might be needed in the future are fired. Travel is cut at the very time that customer contact is most important. And, of course, the time-honored budget cushions—maintenance, training, and education—are thrown overboard along with any vestiges of trust that might remain.

The third strategy isn't very pretty, either, but might be as effective as the others. Acknowledging the hopelessness of the task, managers just tell the budget department, "Do what it takes to put the budget together, then we will fake it to get through the year somehow."

Now, let's complicate the process. Because the evaluation and reward system is usually built around the functions, the budget is built around functions also—usually to the detriment of horizontal issues: products and customers. Marketing requests the money it needs or thinks it can get and allocates it over the products under its purview. Manufacturers do the same—as do distribution and the other line activities. Certainly there are attempts to coordinate these budgets in terms of products or customer groups—the horizontal aspects of the firm—but the budgeting I have observed rarely does this effectively. The functions work in relative isolation. Product managers are generally ineffective at budget time. Product strategy is often submerged by functional considerations, thus suboptimizing the important work of the firm.

Staff activities are usually lumped together, and if activities are spread, they are usually spread against functions. They are not tied to products or customers. Worse, I have yet to talk to a line manager who trusts the allocation process. Now let's complicate the process even more. Say that merit pay or incentive bonuses are tied to performance and that these targets are not only vertical but pushed down to each of the relevant activities in the functions. If trust ever existed, it is banished by this process. The product manager who reports to the marketing vice president believes that he or she is shortchanged on resources or support and is asked to take chances on pricing that may diminish unit sales. Marketing research almost never gets the money it needs. Advertising begins with *A*, so when budgets are adjusted downward, advertising is first in line. Across functions, the wars we have reported on earlier are even more fierce. Salespeople *know* that they can meet their numbers with better marketing support. Marketing *knows* that if the salespeople were more effective, marketing could get more mileage. They are all disquieted if manufacturing causes unscheduled cost increases or is behind schedule. The list is dreary and long. But we keep slogging along.

I know of a superbly run, small family-owned company that in 1991 missed its profit budget—on the high side—by $1 million, about 100 percent. I also know of a large retailer that in the same year missed its budget on the low side by about $40 million—the percentage was astronomical. Both firms use the vertical method of preparing budgets. The smaller firm does a better job of coordinating the functions; nevertheless, the process remains more vertical than horizontal. Both these firms are led by extremely intelligent, knowledgeable executives who spend a significant portion of their time in some aspect of business planning and budgeting. Moreover, some of their support staff spend as much as 50 percent of their time on budgeting activities. Considering the wild variances in their performance against budget, one has to wonder: Why bother with budgeting? Well, there is a better way. Here are some of the guidelines.

- Use the budget for planning, not for control or evaluation. It is a living tool—subject to change, hopefully for the better, but it is not written in stone. (Who in early 1990 predicted Desert Shield?)

- Do not start with financial guidelines such as 15 percent growth and 20 percent return on assets employed. These not only tend to mask real problems that must be faced, but quite often they are limiting, causing loss of strategic opportunities.

- Do not prepare best-case, worst-case budgets. They are confusing. Instead, prepare one budget—the most realistic budget possible at the time. Base it on an unvarnished analysis of the past, an honest look at the present, and a realistic prediction of the future.

- Do prepare the budget by product or by customers—horizontally, not vertically.

- Unless your company is a giant or a conglomerate, start and finish the budget process in one week or less. Bring together all the relevant decision makers and information sources in the same room at the same time—preferably off-campus— with the CEO, who has the responsibility of running the meeting. Be sure the meeting also includes decision support services or MIS professionals, who have their PCs and spreadsheet programs close at hand. To begin the meeting, review the presentations of the financial and budget people who will have prepared graphs showing performance over the past three years. Next open the meeting to anyone and everyone who can add to the understanding of the past performance or who can make suggestions for future improvement. Here the PC operators can begin to play "what if" and "what else" games, in order to sharpen people's thinking. With all this as a background, the CEO and others involved in strategic planning should present their views on the strategic direction of the company in terms of both existing and new products and services. This presentation should serve as a backdrop for general discussion of each of the products and customer groups. Freewheeling is in order at this early stage of the process—questions like, "How could we double the profitability of Product A" or "How can we break through on Product B rather than settle for incremental increases?" Resources needed to accomplish these goals should be discussed in rough numbers. As these suggestions are explored, the decision support people should be gathering information so that in an appropriate time they can produce a rough idea of the financial result of these activities. They will usually need to work during the evening to produce the various scenarios that have been discussed.

These broad, strategic aspects of the budget process are critically important but are usually given short shrift in the traditional process. Only after strategic issues are thoroughly vetted should the focus begin to narrow. When they do narrow, budgets for the important products or product groups should be developed in rough approximations. (Precision in budgeting is nonsense. Financial people who are trained that everything should cross foot and tie in should be advised to loosen up during this planning process.) As the preliminary numbers are rolled up, it becomes clear why all the decision makers and information sources along with the CEO should be in the same room at the same time. Conflicts that arise among product groups and services or between marketing, R&D, purchasing, sales, manufacturing, distribution, and the various support services can be resolved on the spot. A CEO who is well-prepared can smell out and squelch political ploys. These conflicts need not be corrosive. They can be creative under the guidance of an effective CEO. For instance, manufacturing might be incurring costs that were appropriate at one stage but that can now be eliminated. With manufacturing, sales, and marketing in the same room, decisions to remove these costs can be made on the spot. Moreover, if the compensation plan that I proposed in Chapter 5 is in place, then the various players will know that if the firm does well, they will do well also. Therefore, power plays will be diminished.

After the entire product line or range of services has been reviewed, it should be revisited in terms of major customers or customer groups. Any unusual opportunities or resource needs to better serve strategic customers or customer groups can then be cranked into the budget.

Let's say now that the financial and budgeting support people have kept on top of the discussions and are prepared to roll up the rough numbers on the last day of the meeting. Let's say also that when they do, the results are disappointing. Sales are projected to rise by 5 percent, return on sales is down from last year, return on invested capital is disappointing. So be it! If indeed the best efforts of everyone have gone into the process, the budget should not be changed. It should be adopted. *But here, an important distinction should be made. The budget should be adopted, but the outcome should not be embraced.*

The task, then, starting immediately is to begin improving the outcome. This process will focus everyone on stark reality—not gossamer dreams that paper over the tough problems and allow the organization to postpone corrective actions until late in the year.

Then, as these early year improvements are realized, they should be rolled up quarterly into revised budgets that reflect current realities. Or, if improvements cannot be reasonably made—if it is one of those miserable years—but if the company knows that actions it is taking will keep it in business for the future, then so be that also.

There is an important difference between this process and the traditional reforecasting activity. The process described here starts with reality. Real problems are highlighted. The need for immediate creative action is dramatized. Confusion and procrastination caused by reserves for contingencies, best-case, worst-case, and all the other complexities are eliminated. The mission is clear.

The foregoing was to assist those who believe in budgets as a management tool. For iconoclasts, there is another way.

Instead of preparing a budget, identify all the key ingredients of performance, devise a way of keeping these indicators very visible—then through intensive interactive processes across functions, set out to improve on each of these key items...without preparing a final budget. Here is an example: A turnaround that I was involved in was facing a particularly severe financial crisis. I had determined that we did not have time nor should we use our energy to roll up a financial budget. (In this instance, I told the bank that we would be working on cash projections but would not be producing an operating budget or balance sheet. The bankers were visibly upset by my decision. However, inasmuch as the bank had no experience in running the business, as I suggested they might if they had become too insistent, they went along.) There was no budget, but there was a strategy. A clearly articulated strategic thrust was thoroughly argued and well communicated to the key players. It was a dynamic strategy: Crisp predictions in a crisis are not only impossible to achieve but foolish to attempt. But the strategy gave us broad guidelines for resource allocation and operational priorities, and it gave us room to make corrections as we learned where our predictions were wrong. Using the strategy as our guide, we looked at every key task and planned how it could be improved—what resources would be required and what timetable would be realistic. The process was successful. However, it would not have been successful if the effort had been compartmentalized as in traditional budgeting. And it would not have been successful if we had tried to make projections about things that would be happening six months in the future.

This type of planning requires constant interaction of the decision makers and the information sources. But there is very little paperwork. Very few formal measurements, just improvements—and improvements of the right things, because we were integrating our efforts. Far more important, however, we were not frantically trying to make corrections because we had overcommitted. Moreover, because of continual interaction among the key managers, we found new ways to coordinate activities—to help each other with resources and ideas. The process also uncovered some activities that turned out to be surprisingly successful. But had we budgeted traditionally, we could have missed those opportunities. Indeed, the satisficing thrust of the traditional budget process can constrain profitability. In the example just given, we were able in the second year without a budget to produce a 45 percent pretax ROIC; if we had felt the need to lock up a projection, we would have been reluctant to come close to that number.

The budgeting process just described is enhanced by a permeable organization structure and interactive process in an open, trusting environment. But, here's a nice twist—this process can be used to help develop that environment. Because traditional budgeting is so damaging to the concept of interactive processes in an open trusting environment, it was discussed first—and in greater detail—than others which follow, which also deserve our attention.

Meetings

Meetings are a favorite whipping boy, often with good reason. They are sometimes a form of corporate handwringing, scheduled when executives don't know what else to do. Meetings can be a search for goats rather than for solutions, hardly the type of affair that one would be eager to attend. They are often too long, boring, unplanned, unstructured, and produce no visible results other than the schedule for the next meeting. They can be political cauldrons—"Should I keep my mouth shut, or speak only when spoken to, or should I try to take charge? And if I do take charge, will I be saddled with a dozen assignments that I don't have time to do?"

There are meetings for which the purpose, plan, and time are not announced well in advance—with too many participants, some of whom are there to make sure their ox is not gored, or if the ox is gored he is to report immediately to proper authorities. There are meetings for which the meeting leader is not prepared and does not take the pains to help the participants prepare. There are meetings run by leaders who know how to talk but not to listen. There are meetings in which the leader loses control but does not know it because some of the participants have mastered the process of manipulating the outcomes to their own ends. In many instances the meeting's conclusions are "wired," as accurately suspicioned by the participants—further confirming their beliefs that meetings are unnecessary. Admittedly, some meetings are to confirm, not to decide. Others are to inform. Both are legitimate purposes. But most meetings are for the purpose of solving business problems—a fool's errand in the environment just described. In this environment—where truth, trust, information, and solutions go into deep seclusion—the only competence developed is the fine art of self-defense.

The irony is that there are not too many meetings—just too many bad meetings. Meetings are important management processes—where people can develop their own skills by observing others, where they can learn better how their particular function or activity fits into the larger scheme, where information can be imparted, not by a sterile printed page, but by interactive communication—where, indeed, difficult problems can be solved. All this is enhanced where participants trust each other—where there is an open, honest, exchange of opinions and thoughtful consideration of the business issues, regardless of implications to individuals—where participants feel free to "wing it" during the early stages of the meeting, floating seemingly wild ideas without fear of scorn. Alternatively, if a meeting is moving toward a consensus for which a participant has honest doubts, that person feels perfectly free to express those doubts. In this milieu, where precious time is not wasted jockeying for position, more issues are considered, more creative ideas have a chance to see the light of day, and the politically correct but potentially catastrophic decisions may be avoided. Underscoring the importance of candor in the workplace, I have, as a manager or consultant in business turnarounds, observed losses totalling more than $1 billion (yes, I said "billion") in organizations where people, early in the game, either knew absolutely or had strong premonitions about the problem but were intimidated, squelched, or ignored. Look deeply enough into every business holocaust and you would probably find that someone not only knew of the problem but would have been able to present a credible case—a case strong enough to correct the problem in time.

Those who run meetings are often oblivious to the problems described above. One of the finest young executives I know was astonished to learn that his subordinates were critical of his staff meetings. I had suggested that before he adjourned any meeting, he ask the following questions, then make sure they were answered candidly and discussed fully.

What did we learn from this meeting?

What are three ways we could have made this meeting more productive?

It was in response to these questions that the executive I mentioned earlier learned about the criticism of his meetings. Armed with that intelligence, he reduced the number of staff meetings he held and improved those that remained.

Memoranda

As a manager of business turnarounds, I issue the following memo, usually on my first day.

> This is the last memorandum to be written in this organization for thirty days. If you wish to communicate with someone, get up and go see them. If they are too far away, phone them. If you phone them and they don't return your call, phone me.
> Sincerely,
> John Whitney

Admittedly, this is overkill. But it dramatizes the point. Think of the time to consider, draft, dictate, or type a memo—to reread, perhaps to redraft, then send it through the company mail, sometimes to the office next door. Think of the time for the recipient to read and then ponder, to wonder what the "real" meaning might be, then draft a response, making certain that everyone who was copied on the first memo received a copy of the response, and, for safety, distribute also to those who might have received a blind copy. Compare this process with a face-to-face meeting or a telephone conversation. "Marcia, I've got a really great idea about that new distributor discount program that we have been considering." Marcia might respond, in good spirits, "John, that's a lousy idea—and here are the reasons." Whereupon I might respond, "You're right. Well, let's..."

Here, many alternatives and their iterations can be discussed in a matter of minutes—not the days and weeks required with the memo interchange. Important as it is, however, the overriding consideration is not time—it is quality, it is the competence quotient developed in interactive communications instead of sometimes self-serving documents.

"Documentation" is a particularly insidious form of memo writing. A work sampling study in a New England supermarket revealed that store personnel—other than checkers and night stockers—spent more than 50 percent of their time "documenting" events so they could defend their actions to their managers at corporate headquarters. Downtime on the electronic checkout stations was "documented." Shipments from the central warehouse were double-counted and photographed to "document" damaged cartons and short shipments. Direct store delivery from outside suppliers created a paper storm. What should have been a normal reporting process to provide local managers and support people at headquarters with the information for decision making had become a full-scale defensive mobilization. Think of the wasted time! Perhaps senior managers were correct in their implicit assumption that the store managers were incompetent and could not be trusted. But to allow the process to disintegrate to the actions just described confirms that the leaders were reacting to symptoms, not dealing with causes. More importantly, think of the neglected customer. Think of these energies that were used to document activities, which could have been creatively channeled to finding new and better ways of doing business.

If you believe that your organization is being stifled by paperwork, try a moratorium on memos! That will quickly smoke out the bureaucrats and their artifacts. Another tack is to return self-serving memos to the sender with a note, "Perhaps we should discuss this face to face." When the "boss" sends this signal, word gets around. But, of course, neither of these reactions addresses causes for self-serving memos. Any lasting improvement will result from removal of the causes, not from a command or a pointed suggestion.

Financial and Progress Reviews

These are special cases of meetings; and, like most meetings, their ideal use is for information sharing, for genuine learning, for control, or for a combination of these. All are important. But when reviews are for the purposes of control and evaluation of individual performance, and are too frequent or increase in number and intensity, competence is usually in the prisoner's dock. Competence here works both ways. The incompetent leader will be more apt to call for review sessions than the competent (thus confident) leader, who receives and correctly interprets signals from the organization's daily routines. But incompetence anywhere will spawn review sessions. As a new manager of crisis turnarounds, I hold daily progress reviews until I am satisfied that my own competence is becoming adequate and that my associates are also capable of understanding what is to be done and how to do it. As that assessment is made, meeting frequency is reduced. The management crime, of course, is to recognize incompetence, then do nothing about it, except to continue holding review meetings.

Sign-offs

More signatures, less trust—of either motives or competence! Certainly, sign-offs serve as information carriers as well as controls, but when they are required before the fact, then other information sources are inadequate or competence is suspect. Multiple signatures connote that trust is in full retreat. A senior research scientist who controlled a budget in the millions of dollars told me that six months were required for him to get a $3000 personal computer, because signatures were required all the way to the president. He could run a major research effort but was not competent to know whether he needed a PC.

A division president of a company listed on the New York Stock Exchange told me recently that on the first day of his new assignment, he was expected to add his signature to a requisition for an employee's birthday cake. We both wondered if the personnel department was not competent to match the date of the birthday with the purchase of the cake. We also wondered what would have happened if the executive had been out of town. Would the party have been cancelled, or just postponed until next year?

Another senior manager disclosed that three signatures were required for his travel authorizations. There was no question of malfeasance—moreover, he disliked travel intensely, as do most managers. He joked that his hope was that someday his travel request would be turned down. No such luck! And we both marvelled that such controls were necessary if no requests were denied. One of the company's control mavens trumpeted, "You see, it's working. He won't put in a request that we would not approve." Nonsense! I was reminded of the Manhattan lush who confided to me that Scotch whiskey kept the elephants out of his apartment.

Serial, multiple sign-offs are one of the biggest time and money wasters in U.S. business, and they are usually driven by the presumption of incompetence. I have seen task forces of highly paid people stymied for days because an executive who was "in line" was too busy to even read the signature request. Even worse are the executives at the end of the line who know little about what they are signing and ask a dumb question or throw up a roadblock because of their ignorance. Controls are crucial, certainly! But when people that are not involved, only "in line," are required to approve or disapprove something they know nothing about, then the people who are competent lose their sense of responsibility. Deadlines are missed and costs soar. Much of the waste from unnecessary sign-offs and reviews will be revealed by the measurement audit described in Appendix C.

Handoffs

Although many jobs are handled efficiently when tasks are broken into small pieces, performed repetitively, and handed off to the next operation, we often take these mass production techniques to the extreme, particularly in administrative work. The external manifestation of this management practice is the frustration experienced by the customer who is put "on hold," then transferred from department to department, because the people answering the call do not have the information and therefore the competence to resolve the problem. Although not as damaging as loss of customer confidence, the internal costs are also significant. Costs are higher because of delay, loss of continuity, and the need for integration, coordination, and supervision.

Suggested Improvements: Hold a "Miniaudit" of Administrative Procedures

Here are some ideas for improvement that need not wait for the full-fledged audit discussed in Appendix C.

I recently attended a staff meeting of a senior executive of a medium-size NYSE company, in which he asked his colleagues to help him list and discuss their sources of frustration with the administrative process.

The customer service manager pointed out that authorization limits—for customer credit—were too low for the customer service personnel to perform their jobs properly. After a brief discussion, it was determined that customer service representatives were perfectly capable of making most of the decisions that required approval. The authorization limits were raised at that meeting. No further study was required.

Second was a problem with time cards. It had been assumed that corporate policy required two signatures—with the attendant delays, potential for error, and subsequent frustration of the payee. The decision was made at the meeting that henceforth no signatures would be required. Pay would go through on time and cards audited later. In addition, the company executives are now discussing with the union whether time cards are needed.

The third topic was the monthly corporate forecast. Some of the executives had interpreted these as requests for full-blown presentations, when the corporation really needed only a skeleton presentation—particularly if things were on track. The process was simplified and agreed upon during the meeting—not later or after study.

In another discussion, one product had been causing an inordinate number of customer adjustments because of short shipments. Because the manufacturing vice president, the product manager, order entry, and customer service were all in the same room at the same time, the problem was smoked out. Order entry personnel had been using one unit of measure—the plant had been using another. This problem, which had been going on for years almost undetected by everyone but the customer and the customer service personnel, was corrected immediately because of an open, interactive interchange of the parties involved.

I have participated in similar sessions where the following decisions were made:

- Elimination of approval for executive expense accounts.

- Elimination of time clocks.

- Reduction from three to one for the number of signatures required for purchase orders.

- Decision to move to a self-supervised accounts payable department (training started less than two weeks after the decision, fully implemented in 90 days).

- Elimination of approval for travel requests.

- Decision that henceforth all interoffice communication would be oral, handwritten, or put on E-mail.

- Decision that henceforth managers would answer their own phones unless in a meeting. Much of the secretarial force was, in the next 30 days, reassigned to work more suitable to their knowledge and ability.

- Decision to eliminate fancy typesetting and artwork for overhead transparencies used internally. Everyone was given blank sheets and a marker so they could make their own.

- The number of sign-offs required for a manufacturing change reduced from 11 to 3. A decision was made at the meeting, implementation was studied, and the new process was in place in fewer than 60 days.

- Change in access to mainframe computer—password requirements were relaxed for nonconfidential information. Change implemented in one week.

- Here is a technique which has been successful: Along with the notice of the meeting send an agenda which simply states, "We are going to use this meeting to clear out excessive administrative underbrush. Bring to the meeting at least five examples of administrative tasks you believe to be overcomplicated or unnecessary. Be prepared to discuss."

These are just a few of the hundreds of process changes that I have participated in. Success factors are these:

- The CEO or general manager must be committed to process simplification.

- When problems are complex, relevant data must be gathered and analyzed before the meeting. Reams of raw data are useless in a meeting. However, they should be readily available in case of an analysis that might be inadvertently or intentionally biased.

- The meeting should end with a decision: Go, or no go. When it is the consensus of the group (not just one or two special pleaders) that the decision must be postponed, a "date certain" should be set for the decision. Actions required to reach a decision must be agreed on. A "champion" must be assigned the responsibility and given the resources to move the issue to decision.

- An open, trusting, interactive environment is necessary for best results; however, meetings of this type can be used to establish such an environment when it does not exist. As the meetings produce results, the CEO should say to meeting participants, "Go ye and do likewise," with their own direct reports and then ask their associates to do the same, until the process reaches all levels of the organization.

I am now convinced that many of the irksome, time-wasting minutiae in business organizations can be eliminated with the process described above. I further believe that latent disasters can be avoided and that chronic hidden problems can be smoked out.

10

Competence and Constant Improvement of Individuals

People cannot be trusted to do their jobs if they do not know how. And if they have incompetent leaders, the coefficient of mistrust is the number of those leaders multiplied by the number of people who report to them. This calculation—in the context of the degree of incompetence that we observe daily—suggests that the cost of incompetence overwhelms the cost of misalignments, rewards, and measurements—or even the cost of integrity failure, a serious but relatively confined problem.

When organizations address the issue of competence, they usually respond with a training program. But training is only one of the requirements for competence of individuals. Other factors include recruiting, education, and information. Before we address these factors, however, we need to understand the profound change in the relationship of individuals to their organizations just in the last two decades.

Until very recently, trust had been an almost-forgotten word for both the individual and the organization, whereas during the relatively carefree postwar years trust seemed to be a hallmark in this relationship. Times were good. The economy and jobs both were growing. Unemployment was stable. Yes, there were upheavals—in industries as well as in organizations. And there were the inevitable Willy Lomans, symbols of failure of both the organization and the individual. But on balance, people trusted the idea that if they performed well, their jobs were safe, and if they performed exceptionally well, the system would take care of them either in terms of security or advancement. We all know what happened in the mid-1970s through the 1980s and into the 1990s. The downsizings were not just the result of economic cycles. They were structural, long-term adjustments made in response to more effective global competition. Slowly the realization dawned that more productive work was done with fewer people, not because of technology alone but, sometimes more importantly, because of differences in management techniques and work methods. Then came truth's cold shower. Things would never be the same. It was akin to the loss of innocence when the realization dawns that the world is no longer a teddy bear. Trust was now tainted, not only by the plight of the victims but also by the concern of the survivors who were afraid that the next pink slip would be theirs.

In light of the foregoing, how do we now address trust in the context of an interactive, open environment, and the individual's commitment to the aim, vision, mission, and values of the firm? The task is much the same as healing a marriage where one or both parties have been unfaithful—slowly and with care, with modest expectations that celebrate and endeavor to preserve even small improvements, with the realization that the phrase *company loyalty*—either from or to—will not in our lifetimes mean the same things as it did in the seeming halcyon days. With the realization that at first the reactions will be both predictable and damaging: Me first, and to hell with the rest. Certainly not the prescription for a loyal work force eager to commit unbridled energy and creative effort for the good of the enterprise.

But the next reaction is also predictable. People with healthy psyches become uncomfortable with the alienation that is attendant with extreme self-centeredness. They yearn for a new relationship, but one that shelters them from their former vulnerability. They begin to learn how to protect themselves while preserving the new system they join. If things go well, they can then construct relationships that not only will protect and pre-serve but also will enhance. These three descriptors, *alienation* followed by *caution* and concluding with *commitment*, are the framework for the enquiry which follows.

I will argue that the alienation that has occurred during the last two decades has been calamitous and costly, that we will pay the price for several years. Then I will argue that the rela-tionships between the individual and the organization can strengthen and can emerge more productive than before.

First, let us look at the costs. We shall do so in the context of the power and frailty of systems. The output of a system increases almost exponentially after input needs (breakeven) are met. When all the components of a system perform superbly in quest of a common goal, the surplus that is produced can be immense. Moreover, a functioning system has enough compen-satory ability to operate even when one of its components does not perform well. However, that compensatory action puts stress on other components. When, for whatever reason, several parts of the system begin to function improperly, the system is negatively leveraged—until it is destroyed. I do not propose that the current disaffection alone is great enough to destroy businesses that have downsized—for several reasons. First, the input reductions have significantly lowered the breakeven points. Second, our trusty but hoary old motivators, greed and fear, ironically are working for us. People are glad to have jobs and are paying closer attention to their work. But as we shall see later, these gains are sometimes illusory and usually temporary.

Downsizing has produced short-term cost reductions but very little else. Many firms have gone through wave after wave of layoffs, terminations, buyouts, and early retirement programs, yet continue to report miserable results. The reasons, of course, are complex. As was discussed in Chapter 2, the most important reason for failure is that firms have treated downsizing as pure-ly an operational cost-cutting move, when it should be treated also as a strategic move.

The argument that follows was proposed earlier, but it needs reiteration here in the context of the topic presently being dis-cussed. The company should carefully identify the core competencies it needs to preserve and protect in order to compete effectively, not only today but also in the future. In this context, a company should consider its people as assets, not costs, then make certain that these assets are nurtured carefully. Next, the company should excise the waste and complexity that has been identified in this book. Those who are involved in activities and those who are assigned to tasks that are deemed unnecessary for the future of the firm should be reassigned if meaningful jobs are available. Otherwise, these people should be asked to leave, with the bitter realization that their plight is generally no fault of their own. Rather, it is the residue of a misdirected or profligate past where the firm had added people to the payroll heedless of the consequences. Unfair? Certainly! And I believe that managers who have contributed to this condition should be dealt with as swiftly and surely as those who are lower in the hierarchy. But, just as those assets that are important to the firm must be preserved—even if it hurts the financial results in the short term—waste and unnecessary complexity must be excised regardless of the immediate cost, if we are to compete with those who have not made the same mistakes.

With the caveat of preserving the jobs that are important to the future, I believe that restructuring and downsizing should be carried out as quickly as possible. When people are uncertain, they will go through the motions, sometimes even vigorously, but their hearts are not in it, and it shows. They find it difficult to make meaningful plans for the future. Marketing programs flounder, the salespeople lose their zest, latent operations improvements remain latent because no one cares deeply enough to risk change. I have acquaintances in large, well-known firms where people are awaiting the night of the long knives. Precious little work is being done until the night is over and the future course is set. Afterward, there will be some apparent improvement. Assuming that the special charges have been acknowledged, operating productivity will, as a consequence of the cost reductions, seem to improve. But any improvements that are achieved are usually superficial. Moreover, they are relative only to the firm's past performance. They do not necessarily address the firm's future ability to compete with organizations that are not only lean but also have a competent work force that is deeply committed to the aim, vision, values, and goals of the enterprise.

Sometimes we in the United States are slow, but we sure aren't dumb. We are finally learning that we cannot save our way to success if what we also save is a suspicious, dispirited work force. Our troubled business giants are slowly learning from entrepreneurial firms that have been doing it right all along. They are learning about the power of a competent work force that is not just doing the same old thing harder and faster. These firms are cutting waste and eliminating unnecessary complexity, not by mandate but by listening carefully to employees across functions and at all levels. These firms are moving controls closer to the work. Slowly, they are questioning and correcting some of the corrosive practices in rewards and evaluation systems that pit people against each other rather than direct energies to the customer. Some of the firms are beginning to understand variation, not just on the shop floor but also in administrative practice. These changes will not only improve the firm's ability to flourish but will assist in the development of a competent work force. Over time, this type of work force will transform the equation between employer and employee. This transformation will play a powerful role in the company of the future.

Ironically, the postwar trusting environment that was described earlier was doomed at the outset, not only because of global competition but because of the imbalance of power. Harsh as it may sound, there was almost a master-slave relationship between employer and employee. The implicit paradigm was command and control. Perhaps a safer term is *paternalism*. The rules were clear. Everything was fine as long as people did what they were told.

The trade union movement sought to redress the imbalance, but it was fatally flawed. With unions on the scene, we had two paternalistic relationships—company and worker, union leader and worker. Furthermore, the triad that this produced directed the focus away from the organization and its customer to a power relationship among the three groups—company, worker, and union leadership (which of course had its own power-seeking agenda). Three-party marriages might work in some societies, but I am not aware of any successes in ours. And one wonders what happened to the troika of another political economy.

Another unfortunate outcome of the trade union movement was the concept of limited competence. Rigid work rules, confining job descriptions, and negotiated productivity increases destroyed the climate for meaningful learning or improvement.

The quality movement and the exigencies of survival have prompted some managers and workers to drag union leaders, kicking and screaming, into a new relationship. The reluctance of union leaders is understandable. They will be superannuated if there is redress in the balance of power between managers and employees. To be fair, I am aware of some instances where union leaders have taken the initiative, but in my experience, these have been the exception, not the rule. There is another very serious impediment to redressing the imbalance of power and influence—senior and middle managers who are uncomfortable in any relationship other than master-slave, command and control. These, too, are facing the fate of the dinosaur. For to survive, companies have no choice but to hire and develop a competent work force that uses not only its arms and legs but also its brains. When this happens, the genie is out of the bottle. The modern, competent work force will not long tolerate an environment or a middle management that minimizes their contribution or stifles their growth. Learning is addictive, and it is the only employee benefit that is vested immediately. The new work force will understand the career advice I give to my students: "Forget the money, the position, or title—they will take care of themselves. But when you stop learning, leave. Otherwise you will become stale and sour. By staying on, you will be doing a disservice to yourself and to the firm." But if you continue to learn, you will always be in demand, and you can usually name your own price.

Some pundits are predicting that this scenario means the death of trust and loyalty. Opportunistic workers will be hopping from job to job, caring only for themselves, heedless of the needs of the firm. And some firms are pouring gasoline onto that fire with their pronouncements that henceforth part-timers will make up a significant portion of their work force. Ostensibly, this will give the firm flexibility and will save costs of health and other benefits. The first mistake is the attempt to repeal the no-free-lunch law of economics. Someone, somewhere, somehow, will pay for the benefits. Chances are that the cost will end up in the hourly rates. The second problem is more serious. People are fooling themselves who think they can achieve the same productivity and quality from a part-time work force that is achievable from a well-led team of competent professionals—a team that has sorted out relationships with one another, that knows what to do, how to do it, when and where to do it, and why to do it.[1]

Let me suggest another scenario—a possibility, not necessarily a probability—that could occur with the right leadership. Contrary to the pundits' fears, trust and loyalty can be enhanced by a competent, independent work force—if management understands the new equation. The strongest bonds are among those who are free to leave but who stay because they are enriched by the encounter and fulfilled by contributing something of value to an organization or to society. The bonds of coercion are the ones that will most surely be severed.

If I were leading a company today, I would communicate as clearly as I could that I expect everyone to simultaneously improve their own marketability by handling challenging assignments, by learning new skills, and by improving their general knowledge. I would tell them that not only are they free to leave, but if they should leave they would be welcomed back. I would then work with them to articulate a vision that would pull us toward a goal that would ensure that the enterprise and all those who were in it were enriched. Then I would make that work so rewarding that people would not think of leaving. This vision is not as utopian as it might sound. The business press regularly reports on companies or divisions which have successfully embraced this or a similar philosophy. Chaparral Steel, Microsoft, Apple Computer, certainly in the early days, Nucor Steel, the Shreveport Truck Division of General Motors, particularly during the early and mid-1980s, the simultaneous engineering group at Caterpillar Tractor, the Zytec Corporation, the Zebra Team at Kodak, the Cadillac Development Team at General Motors. I'm aware that some of these companies are treading on the edge of disaster, but it is instructive to note the attempts to improve by various pockets of excellence. I am aware, also, that success carries its own seeds of destruction, and that chance and fortune also play a role in success and failure. Nonetheless, the examples are ubiquitous, and the logic is compelling. Companies with a competent work force that is dedicated to a common purpose will generally prevail over those with a work force that is less competent and is constrained by a towering hierarchy and torn apart by divisive measurement and reward systems. Now, in the light of the foregoing, let's examine three of the topics that were introduced earlier: recruiting, education, and training.

Hiring and Recruiting

Some organizations recruit only the top 10 percent of the graduating class. ("Serves them right," grumbles Dr. Deming.) I am aware of no study that correlates grades with job performance. One study in the 1960s concluded that good grades in high school predicted good grades in college, which in turn should predict good grades in graduate school (where grades should be good by virtue of the selection process). Perhaps grades predict the ability to study. But that is only one of the requirements for business success.

At hourly or salaried levels, we hire on demonstrated skills. Drill press or lathe operators, of course, need to know how to operate their equipment, and typists should know how to type or run a word processor. Professionals needs to demonstrate certification, and technicians should be able to demonstrate their skills. These requirements, along with the traditional personnel screens, will get the applicant an interview. From that point, however, the criteria in the section of hiring and promotion in Chapter 5 should take over, with the special focus on the person's ability to work productively with others in an environment characterized by trusting relationships. This does not mean that one person should be a clone of the others. Diversity is a requirement of systems. But the following questions should be asked: Does the recruit exhibit a history or a future willingness to learn constantly, a willingness to take on new tasks? Can the person function in an open environment, or does he or she need authoritarian leadership? Did the interviewee agree with everything you said during the interview, or did she or he question or take exception to some? Was the person interviewed by potential coworkers? Their evaluation is particularly important if the prospect is potentially a member of their team or task force, although their evaluation should not be dispositive as to whether he or she is hired. Spotting talent is an unusual skill—sometimes an art—and seeking consensus might be necessary ultimately to implement changes but not necessarily to foster change. Ted Levitt summed it up succinctly—as he always does—with the observation, "Leaders produce consent. Others seek consensus."[2] So the hiring decision is an amalgam of council and counsel and is for the purpose of infusing new skills, insights, and energy into the organization. If this results in an organization that has richer human resources than opportunities for growth, so be it. The people who leave but who have been enriched by the encounter will thank you for it—assuming you handled the separation with care. And the organization will have a rich resource of friends, a resource of which there is never a surfeit.

Education

Three aspects of education will be discussed in this section: entry level, continuing business education, and pursuit of a liberal education.

Entry Level

Clearly, basic education is a most important social issue for U.S. business in the twenty-first century. Without a work force that can read, write, add, and subtract, we will have no choice but to ultimately revert to an eighteenth-century agrarian economy. Although we are now making headway in our ability to compete worldwide, we will grind to a halt unless we can improve the quality of the work force available for entry-level positions in the future.

Until now, business has been "getting by" through very selective hiring practices, but in some areas of the country the entry-level pool of qualified candidates is depleted. The preceding discussion on recruiting notwithstanding, businesses are finding that they now must hire people for entry-level jobs that they wouldn't have dreamed of hiring during the 1970s and 1980s. So, when I advance the proposition "If we can trust everyone to do their jobs correctly—on time—what would an organization structure look like?" some managers do not know whether to laugh or cry. Indeed, if we cannot improve the quality of the entry-level work force, the central theme of this book might have to be modified. Without competence, trust is impossible. If it comes to that, we will need more, not fewer, supervisory personnel.

Continuing Business Education

Here I am differentiating education and training. Furthermore, I am differentiating education the employee brings to the company and the education supported by the company. I use the word *supported* purposely because my Puritan instincts suggest that for certain types of education, not directly related to job performance, employees should share the cost.

"Why bother with education or training?" I have heard some executives say. "There's no loyalty anymore. Why should I spend my money to educate them for another company?" This seemingly poverty-stricken remark carries both irony and merit. The irony is of course that turnover may be the result of the company's policies which do not help the employees grow into better jobs. The merit of the argument stems from the uneven quality of business education. Some management education programs are superb; others are flawed. There are not enough qualified instructors. And too often they are teaching the wrong thing, especially in finance, accounting, organizational theory, general management, and human relations. Changes in the business environment have eclipsed instructors who rely on books instead of current knowledge or experience. Many instructors have not heard of time compression, reengineering, just-in-time, cellular manufacturing, resource-based accounting, activity-based accounting. Many are teaching organization structure as if the traditional functional organization were going unchallenged by process- and product-driven organization structures. They're teaching without fully understanding the nuances of concepts like MBO (management by objectives), MBE (management by exception), incentive compensation plans, and the annual merit review. Yet there is a raging debate in the leading-edge businesses about the application of these concepts.

Some finance teachers teach DCF (discounted cash flow) and NPV (net present value) uncritically, yet these tools are flawed if used woodenly without a view to the company's strategy. Some instructors, who are only seven or eight years behind, are teaching that all the free cash flow of the company should go to service debt.

These flaws are not the exclusive property of small schools that are trying to stay alive by selling executive education and management training. Many of our large research universities make the same mistakes—only better. A young professor cannot get promoted without poking around in the past, piling up citations from luminaries who published years ago. Furthermore, promotion criteria are so demanding that the researcher must stay in a narrowly prescribed specialty. He or she often walks into a classroom terrified that the students will want to extend or expand the discussion beyond the instructor's specialty. Yet the managers who are being taught need to know how that specialty relates to other things they are doing.

Some large companies are dealing with this situation by developing their own management training at their own facilities. Although they hire outside professors, they closely monitor what the professors teach and how they teach it. This raises the possibility that the resulting education may be too narrowly focused, but it nevertheless addresses the education's relevance to the company's aims and values. It also answers the problem of quality. If a company spends its money on education, it should spend it with the same care it does for any other expense or investment. Senior managers should sit in classes to monitor the quality. Better still, managers should spend time with the instructors to find out what they know and how they plan to teach. Managers should make clear their own expectations. If the instructor seems fairly well qualified but is unaware of some special concept that should be taught, the company can point the instructor to the sources of information so the material can be integrated into the course. However, the outside view of a qualified instructor is also important. "Guidance" from the company should not stifle new ideas. In any event, the shortage of good instructors is no excuse for poor business education. There's always a shortage of talent. The successful company finds it or develops it. Whatever firms do, they should not treat the education budget as a necessary evil—budget for it and turn it over to a manager who does not have ready access to senior management. Education is too expensive to ignore.

Liberal Education

Employees sometimes wish to pursue a liberal education which they may not have had the opportunity or motivation to pursue before they started their business careers. Although benefit to the company may seem remote, it seems reasonable that the company contribute to this endeavor. Shakespeare's history plays teach more about leadership than many of the modern books on the subject. Much of the great literature deals with ethics or dilemmas of choice, certainly relevant to today's business and the central argument of this book. Philosophers, poets, and psychologists speak to the issues of individuals and their responsibilities to groups. However, it isn't necessary to reach for direct benefits to justify this type of education. People who have had the gumption and grit to better themselves, partially at their expense using their own time, usually will be more productive employees or managers.

Training

Have you ever stood in a supermarket line whose checkout person was a new hire without adequate training? The seemingly interminable wait provides time for reflection and analysis. For instance, you may note that the line next to you is moving twice as fast as yours. A simple calculation reveals that the company is losing 50 percent productivity. With nothing else to do, you might then compare the productivity loss with the cost of training off-line. But you might then reflect that both the trainer's and the trainee's salaries would offset the productivity gains of proper training. In many companies, the analysis stops there. If benefits are not as easily measurable as those in the checkout example, the conclusion may be, "Training costs too much money. Besides, the turnover is horrendous. We just can't afford to train someone who probably will leave, so just put the new hire next to an experienced checker and make sure that the front-end manager is there to help."

Here again we encounter one of the fundamental flaws in modern management theory, which says that we should measure minutiae. The calculation of direct productivity loss compared to the cost of training is relatively easy to measure but cannot reflect all the intangibles and imponderables.

How much productivity is lost in the adjoining lines because the "trained checkers" have to stop to answer the trainee's questions? How much productivity was lost in the entire front-end operation because the manager was doing on-line training and remedial work rather than dealing with customers and helping ensure the normal flow? How much productivity is lost forever because the new checker's clumsy efforts will become his or her norms? Once a person reaches a stable state in a skill, no amount of retraining will help. It's too late.[3] How much will be lost because of misrings? How much will be lost because the poorly trained checker will not know correct prices on perishable items, which are not scanned, or items without prices or bar codes? Study after study confirms that when checkers guess, they guess too low—they learn early on about the wrath of a customer who feels that he or she has been overcharged.

How do we measure costs when we look at this situation through the customer's eyes? What is the consequence if the checker, frightened and frustrated, becomes defensive—the friendly smile turns to a sullen silence? Now the customer is dealing with both loss of time and discourtesy. If there is a better alternative, the customer will find it. In metropolitan New York City there are few alternatives, so the customers become adversaries. Breakage and shrinkage go up. Items picked up in one part of the store are left on counters two aisles away. In-store circulars are dropped on the floor. Merchandising in the dairy case is in disarray because the customers, who by now don't trust anything, are looking for the best date on the carton. Arguments break out at the slightest provocation. The store manager as well as the front-end manager spend hours dealing with disgruntled customers and antagonistic employees. How does one measure these losses?

Is this example far-fetched? Not at all. A supermarket chain's stores in New Jersey and Long Island that are close by Manhattan count at least 25 percent of their weekend business from fugitives from Manhattan checkout counter wars.

But we still haven't counted all the costs. Checkout personnel turnover runs as high as 150 to 200 percent in the New York City area. Think of the management time and direct cost to interview, to set up the payroll records, and to handle other administrative paraphernalia.

More than 60 percent of the shrinkage (loss of gross margin caused by theft, damage, and obsolescence) is attributable to employees. In every case I have studied, the lower the morale, the higher the shrinkage. Although morale problems are not solely a function of training, the jungle just described certainly produces low morale of customers and employees alike.

Without realizing it, managers in this milieu get trapped in a vicious cycle. As more things go wrong, more procedures, controls, and systems are overlaid on an already complex system. More and more time is spent for policing, inspecting, cajoling, threatening, or documenting incidents so that the person can be dismissed with the hope that the lawsuit for wrongful dismissal will be won.

The problems just described are not reserved for supermarkets in New York City. One troubled national women's clothing chain reported a 265 percent turnover of sales clerks and an 89 percent turnover of store managers last year. The direct costs of this charade are overwhelmed by the loss of sales from clerks and managers trying to find their way around rather than address the needs of the customer.

Banks and financial institutions generally spend more time and money than retailers on training. But too often training is perfunctory. In one Midwest savings and loan which I studied several years ago, only 35 percent of the tellers knew what percentage meant—yet the customers routinely asked, "What percent am I earning now?"

On two occasions, I have suggested to senior executives of large banks that they should train lending officers to analyze strengths and weaknesses of businesses and business management, as well as to make loans. Their first response was, "We're already doing that." When I asked if that were why banks had performed so well in the last decade, they fell back on, "It would cost too much money." When I asked them to compare potential training cost increases with last year's loan losses, they fell silent.

Of course, money for training is not the only answer. Too often the effectiveness of training is equated with the size of the budget. Wrong! Money is not the issue if training is delegated to some well-meaning training director who is so far removed from senior management and line operations that the content of the training is off the mark. Just as wrong, however, is the converse: "Send George out on the line and let Joe train him." In all likelihood, Joe was trained by Jill who was trained by Jim who was trained by Janet. As Dr. Deming is fond of pointing out, worker training worker without supervision is like mixing paint to match the last bucket you used rather than the first. You may start out with blue and end up with green. Joe may be doing the job wrong; he may be slow and sloppy; he may not care to spend his time training someone else. And even if he wanted to, he may not know how to train. Although the point is made elsewhere in this book that no one knows more about the job than the person doing it, it does not follow that he or she is doing it as well as it should be done or that he or she is an acceptable trainer. For training to be effective, it should be pedagogically sound, should teach best practices, and should reflect the aims, values, missions, and objectives of the company. And, as is the case in education, senior management must be intensely involved. Training is too important to be delegated.

Conclusion

11

The Trust Factor: From Theory to Practice

People in business have been heard to say, "Those who can't do, teach." Academics have said, "Those who can't teach, do." A colleague of mine once quipped, "Whitney, you're in terrible shape. Those who can't do either, do both." My colleague's jibes notwithstanding, I suggest that balance is required. Theory without action is fruitless, and action without theory is often mindless.

I understand why practical managers want solutions as quickly as possible: Time is of the essence. But the antecedents to solutions are problems. Until problems are well defined, they defy solutions. Moreover, the same problems will crop up over and over again unless their causes are understood. These causes usually are the results of the underlying theory that guides our actions. Enduring change, therefore, requires a theory change. It requires also that we be able to distinguish good theory from bad theory—useful concepts from harmful concepts. Moreover, enduring change requires that our faulty concepts be discarded and replaced. Overlaying one on the other might mask the problem, but will not solve it.

Good theory not only helps us to gain understanding of problems, it eliminates problems. Moreover, it is the beacon that leads us most directly to our destination. It is the glue that holds the enterprise together, that gives cohesion to and directs the implementation of its strategies. Good theory is not ephemeral. It does not embrace fads and panaceas. But neither is it static. It changes as the enterprise and its people grow in wisdom. In this context, theory is nurtured and reshaped by debate, by new ideas, and by new insights.

Bad theory is also powerful and enduring. It causes us to make the same mistakes over and over again. It is particularly powerful when we do not realize that it is bad. It sometimes is so ingrained in our thoughts and actions that we do not recognize it. In some instances we confuse this faulty theory with conventional wisdom or common sense—both of which tell us that the world is flat. For instance, here are a few of the concepts that seem harmless enough but are in fact underlying causes of mistrust.

- Business is zero-sum. For every winner there must be a loser.
- If competition is good, cooperation is bad.
- Competition inside the firm should be like competition outside the firm.
- If you can't measure it, you can't manage it.
- We can always measure performance.
- We should pay for performance.
- Numbers tell the story.
- Only the bottom line is important.
- If you never have a bad month, you'll never have a bad year.
- The truly effective person is dependent on no one but himself.
- "That's marketing's job"—or manufacturing, or distribution, et cetera.
- Most people are untrustworthy and incompetent. They must be supervised closely, and their work must always be inspected.
- The job of the manager is to control.
- No one should have more than six people reporting to him or her.
- Approval must go through the chain of command.

- Information must go through the formal channels of communication.
- To make sure it is understood, write it down.

The propositions above, presented in the context of this book, are not a pretty sight. Yet, standing alone, they can be beguiling. Each seems germane for some situations. Many are commonly accepted as sound management theory. I have heard each of them in one form or another during the past year. But when they become operational, it is soon apparent that the good they might provide is overcome by the waste and unnecessary complexity they create.

Because criticism carries the responsibility for remedy, I have proposed a general theory that should do much to eliminate the causes of mistrust and its attendant problems. In essence, the theory is:

A business is a complex system of interdependent parts. Managing its complexity requires competent individuals working within a permeable organization structure, using interactive processes in an open, trusting environment. When performance evaluation and rewards do not reflect the interdependence of the components, and when the system's performance is affected by incorrect or misleading information, mistrust is created. This mistrust creates waste and needless complexity. Moreover, mistrust dilutes efforts and misdirects creative energy from the real work of the enterprise—to design, produce, sell, distribute, and collect for a product or service that gets and keeps profitable customers.

Conversely, trust in the fairness of the evaluation and reward system, trust in the competence of colleagues and the organization, trust in the information that the organization and its people produce, and trust in the integrity of the organization and its people reduces waste and complexity. When these conditions apply and when people in the enterprise understand, believe in, and willingly support its aim, mission, values, goals, and objectives, creativity will flourish, costs will plummet, profits will soar. The organization's ability to survive and grow is enhanced. The vitality of the enterprise and its people is enriched.

Putting new theory into practice is not easy. But the stakes are high. Businesses that are carrying the burden of mistrust will have difficulty competing. Revolutionary changes are cropping up all over the world. Hierarchical structures are being dismantled. Traditional staff and administrative positions are being eliminated. Companies that conduct business as usual are finding that structural cost inefficiencies, poor quality, and the inability to swiftly change direction are threatening their existence. The need for change is dramatic.

Although some of the ideas here might have seemed strange in earlier decades, they have been made familiar by companies, global and domestic, which now realize that the old ways have bottled up the true potential of a company's finest assets—its people. Companies everywhere are using some of the techniques here—task forces, teams, concurrent engineering, and re-engineering, among others. However, some of these firms are beginning to realize that techniques alone are insufficient. They are beginning to understand that enduring change and sustainable improvement require a change in the underlying theory—the assumptions and concepts that guide the enterprise.

The following are suggestions—not prescriptions—about how one might proceed to adopt the theory that has been proposed. Although these suggestions need not be addressed serially, or woodenly, each of them should be considered.

- Dramatize the need for change.
- Identify those problems that do not seem to go away.
- Identify the symptoms of recurring problems.
- Understand the difference between symptoms and apparent causes.
- Understand the differences between apparent and real causes.
- Adopt the theory that will address the real causes.

Dramatize the Need for Change

Business theory and practice will not change until the need is acknowledged. Too often, the need is not acknowledged until a crisis appears. Ironically, managing change in crisis is relatively easy—survival is easy to dramatize. But leaders of businesses that are not in crisis or those that are in crisis but do not yet realize it have a more difficult task.

One way to dramatize the need is to make certain that people in the organization discuss thoroughly and understand the anatomy of failures at companies like General Motors, IBM, Kodak, Compaq Computers, the big banks, the big retailers, and the host of others that once seemed invincible but ran into trouble in the mid-1980s and early 1990s.[1] One or more of these cases might provide a basis for comparison of your own practices and policies. If this exercise does not expunge complacency, ask yourself and your colleagues to list all your customers whose business you have lost totally or partially during the last year. Next, list the customers who have been giving signals that they might soon defect. Then, list all the proposals for new business that have been unsuccessful. Finally, list and honestly discuss the reasons why. If, for instance, the primary reason is price, you probably want to disabuse yourselves of the notion that the competitors are losing money on every order but making it up on the volume. Chances are that their costs are lower. Chances are also that their product or service is better or better tailored to the customer needs. A day of hard-nosed, brutally frank analysis of the reasons for lost opportunities along with a detailed discussion of competitive strengths might dramatize the need for change.

Identify Problems That Do Not Seem to Go Away

How often have you fixed a problem only to find that it crops up again—perhaps in a slightly different guise, but the same problem nevertheless. To dramatize the need for profound change, identify those problems that seem immutable and intractable, then discuss why they are so difficult to solve. It will soon become clear that these are the problems most in need of new theory. For instance:

- Why can't we reduce the time-to-market for new products and services?
- Why do we consistently miss our sales projections?
- Why is it that rejects, rework, and scrap are consistently higher than our competitors?
- Why are we always surprised about time and cost overruns?
- Selling, general, and administrative expenses as a percentage of revenues are supposed to go down as revenues go up. Why are ours going the other way?
- We have downsized three times. Why aren't we profitable?
- Why are financial reports always late?
- Why do people say we have too many meetings?
- Why do our management meetings always seem to end up in arguments?
- Why do we lose the people we want to keep and keep the people we want to lose?
- Why won't people stay after hours or on weekends when we really need them?
- Why is absenteeism consistently high?

The list is depressingly familiar. It is also depressingly long because it identifies profound problems. Worse, it is depressingly short because it lists only a few of the problems that exist.

The example that will be used in the rest of this analysis is the first one listed above—*the time-to-market problem*. This example is based on my observations of several such projects, both as a consultant and as a CEO. Although this case addresses introduction of a new product, the process works equally well for services. It works also for internal administrative changes.

Identify the Symptoms of Recurring Problems

Recognizing symptoms before they become serious problems is imperative. However, symptoms are sometimes mistakenly characterized as problems. When this happens, there is a tendency to settle for superficial remedies. By treating the following issues as symptoms merely, not real problems, we are more apt to stay on track in our quest for real causes and their solutions.

Here are just a few of the symptoms that I have observed that create delays in time-to-market:

- Arguments between people in design, marketing, purchasing, manufacturing, and administration.
- Design insists, "No more changes."
- Marketing wants even more features.
- Purchasing disagrees with design's materials specifications.
- Manufacturing wants the time to make its own drawings and develop its own specifications.
- The CFO wants more time to approve the capital expenditure requests.
- The product manager sits on the final proposal for two weeks.
- The toolmaker insists that design changes would yield important savings.

Understand the Differences between Symptoms and Apparent Causes

The symptoms above reflect deeper problems. On occasion these deeper problems are real causes. More often, however, they serve only to enrich our understanding of the symptoms. They are the apparent causes. Here are some that apply to the time-to-market example:

- Manufacturing believed that the new product would be difficult and expensive to make.
- Purchasing believed sincerely that if it had been brought in early, savings could have been realized in material and component costs.

- Marketing believed that the others are not sensitive to the market.
- The others believed that people in marketing were impractical—thought only about sales, ignored costs.
- CFO not only had a capital constraint but was worried about increases in inventory that new products would create.
- Personnel department needed more time to study the ramifications of the new product on the present labor contract.
- Tool designers and outside suppliers believed they had important contributions to make.
- There were few group discussions. During the entire cycle, arguments were carried on, primarily through written reports and memoranda, with their attendant time losses.

Understand the Differences between Apparent Causes and Real Causes

The problems described above are serious. They need attention. But they do not address the roots of the problems. Solving any one or all of these in absence of theory change will "scotch the snake, not kill it," as Macbeth said after he did away with Duncan.

It should come as no surprise that the real culprits—the root causes of the time-to-market problem—are, in part, the causes that I have discussed throughout the book:

- Concern about the evaluation and reward system.
- Little trust in the competence of others.
- Failure to realize the interdependence of functions as parts of a larger system.
- Mistrust and consequent disregard for information.
- Concern about the motives, if not the integrity, of others.

Evaluation and Rewards. Clearly the evaluation and reward system is at work. Each of the functional goals is in some way detrimental to others. To get unit costs down and productivity up, manufacturing needs a small number of simple products and long production runs. Moreover, changes that are made in midstream make it difficult for manufacturing to cover its fixed costs. Marketing wants a variety of "stand-out" products and short runs to provide flexibility in order to meet customer order patterns. The purchasing department is measured not on the quality or performance of the product, nor on the total cost of production, but on purchase price variance. Finance would not mind the low costs in manufacturing, but might dislike the long runs and the high inventory levels that they imply. These are just the tip of the iceberg. Down in the nuts and bolts of everyday decision making, hundreds more just like this occur daily in companies all over the world. Indeed, the phrase "misalignment of measurements and rewards" was not my creation. It is the phrase that was used over and over again by a major U.S. firm's hourly workers and middle managers who were members of a "problem-solving group" that was trying to find ways to reduce time-to-market. These people realized that they could not make fundamental, enduring change when their efforts were evaluated vertically—by function, rather than horizontally—in this case, by product. Until the fundamental problem of measurement and reward is corrected, symptoms might be treated, some apparent problems might be solved, but the root causes will remain and similar problems will surface.

Competence. Let's look at this issue now in terms of competence. The primary criterion for competence—a permeable organization, using interactive processes in an open, trusting environment—was not being met by the time-to-market problem-solving groups that I observed. The managers had been accustomed to the one-off, hand-off routine. All communications were written. Documentation was pervasive—and not in the productive sense (preserving that which is useful) but in the political sense—each of the functions wanting to protect itself from blame if things went wrong or to cover itself with glory if things went right. Individual competence, of course, is fundamental. If the people do not know how to do their jobs and have no opportunity for improvement, no amount of management theory can help them.

Systems. Throughout these development cycles, neither the leaders nor the managers of the various functions demonstrated that they really understood their interdependence—that they were all part of a larger system. Most of the leaders' interventions were on a one-off basis with the functional heads, who generally had firm and fixed ideas about their own functional responsibilities. Accordingly, when the various functional heads met as a group, the leader rarely was able to build a bridge across their activities. When the leader was able to persuade one function to make a change which would facilitate the work of another function, the change was seen as a compromise. The manager who agreed to the change characterized the agreement as a debt that would require repayment at a future date. The irony, of course, is that each of these managers was being paid by the same company—a company that ran the risk of failure if its new products were late or unsuccessful.

Compare the process above to an open, free-flow exchange of ideas that could shape a new product if marketing people, designers, purchasing managers, manufacturing managers, tool and die makers, and key suppliers would come together with a common aim—to quickly bring to market the finest products they could build. Next, compare their subsequent actions in the normal course of product development, where adjustments are nearly always required. Product teams that do not act in the free-flowing interactive manner just described usually will require more time and will develop products that are not as well suited to the market as teams that see themselves as inter-active systems with a common aim.

Information. I reported earlier the instance in which manufacturing managers developed their own drawings and specifications, effectively discarding those that had previously been prepared by the designers. When information is deemed untrustworthy, time-to-market as well as cost and quality are nearly always the victims. Other examples abound. I call some of them "functional piecemeal"—the arcane jargon of finance and accounting mixed in with terminology from marketing, manufacturing, and distribution—all combined to create the corporate version of the Tower of Babel. Information that is essential to the enterprise is drowned by the detail. We have too much information presented in inappropriate formats to too many people at inappropriate times. Delays created by the search for relevant data are a big factor in time-to-market delays. Information cannot be presented in a vacuum. Reports of performance, whether of individuals, mechanisms, divisions, or products, need to be made in the context of the system in which they exist. Specific suggestions about improving the usefulness of information have been made in Chapter 6 and in Appendix C.

Integrity. I saw no examples of integrity failure in the cases I have just reported. Suffice it to say, however, when people's motives are dramatically different, integrity is often at risk. The recommendations I have made do not address the issue of inherent integrity, but they do assist in keeping integrity failure to a minimum in the workplace.

Adopt the New Theory That Will Address Real Causes

One thing is certain. Organizational trust will not be automatically realized by virtue of a CEO's pronouncement that "Henceforth we will all trust each other." The concept of improved trust introduced in this manner will meet the same fate as empowerment—a magnificent idea that has been trivialized by a lack of understanding of its requirements and by the ironic notion that it will be adopted as a result of the cascade approach—flowing like a stream from the CEO source to the sea of humans that must make it work. The contrary is true, of course. The adoption of any new theory requires the understanding, commitment, and leadership of the CEO and the senior managers. But meaningful change also requires thoughtful discussion by everyone who will be affected. Otherwise, the new concept might seem to be adopted, but at the first sign of trouble people will discard it for the comfort of the devils they know. Indeed, exorcism of harmful past practices is imperative for sustenance of new practices. At a minimum, the five causes of mistrust should be confronted. Other causes that are specific to the organization should also be addressed. Here are three suggested approaches. They are suggestions only. Every organization is different and should develop the change method most suited to its needs.

The approach that follows naturally from this discussion is to identify one or two of the firm's seemingly intractable problems, then to use the steps that are suggested in the time-to-market example as a diagnostic tool. The diagnosis will usually prescribe the treatment, particularly if the leaders have committed to the removal of the causes of mistrust. As I have emphasized earlier, and will reiterate, the discussions should ultimately include most, if not all, of the people who will be affected. Their participation in the exploration of differences between symptoms and apparent causes, and the differences between apparent causes and root causes, will lay a firm foundation for change.

Another company's successful effort started with the leader and his 14 direct reports. These managers spent the better part of two days discussing the topic, "What do I do that makes your job more difficult?" Each of these 14 senior executives and the CEO took their turns in the barrel. An outsider was present to record the issues that surfaced and to keep the process on track. Trust was not specifically mentioned at first, but it soon emerged as a central issue. The sometimes argumentative discussions highlighted the classic interfunctional stresses—onerous reporting requirements from the controller's office; the time-worn problems of the product manager who has very little agency power but who nevertheless needs to marshall the resources of design, manufacturing, sales, marketing, and distribution; the daily squabbles among sales, manufacturing, and distribution in their efforts to juggle relatively inflexible schedules with traditionally imprecise forecasts. Well over 100 specific sources of conflict were documented. Some of the stresses that were identified were inevitable. When this was the case, the discussion centered not on how the stresses could be removed, but how they could be ameliorated. In other cases, festering wounds were treated on the spot. Actions were taken to remove the problems with the caveat that actions which were taken that affected people or activities not represented at the meeting would later be discussed or confirmed with those who were affected. But nearly all the stresses were related to the five causes of mistrust. The discussion set the stage for their removal or modification.

Another widely reported and successful endeavor was the profound change made by an electronics distributor headquartered on the west coast and listed on the New York Stock Exchange.[2] The COO and CEO had pondered over Dr. Deming's theories, and had identified dozens of examples of egregious waste that was caused by the various incentive programs for salespeople. Additionally, they were concerned about the amount of time spent and frustration created by the administration of other incentive and bonus plans. Finally, one day they decided, "Let's just do it." Salespeople were put on salary, individual incentive and merit programs were replaced by across-the-board profit sharing. The company's leaders also addressed other causes of mistrust. Information about the company's activities and financial performance was more widely disseminated, boundaries between functions were blurred, and the company began acting as a system. These changes helped the company to quickly develop new services which are redefining the nature of their business, moving it from a commodity distributor to a high-value-added supplier. The company, which had been profitable before the change, became even more profitable. Furthermore, prospects for the future seem excellent. The leaders believe that the dramatic changes they made have played an important role in their success.

In this case, the company announced the change before making extensive preparation. But once they introduced the change, they put forth heroic efforts to implement it. This approach of announcing the change first, then implementing it, has worked well for the electronics distributor, confirming my earlier assertion that there is no "best way" for everyone.

The company's leaders must tailor their efforts to fit the company's own circumstances.

Regardless of the approach, two caveats should be reiterated. These will apply regardless of the change method that is employed.

Removal of the five causes of mistrust will not be easy. The organization cannot merely wave a wand and decree that henceforth everyone will be competent, that information will be relative, timely and trustworthy, that the differential merit pay and incentive pay will be replaced by a universal bonus plan. Some of these will take time—for instance, improving the competence level of individuals. Others, like the pay plans, will meet resistance from managers who feel that pay plans are necessary adjuncts to control. However, free-flowing and vigorous debate will bring a sharp focus to these areas of concern and resistance, and will help to prescribe how they should be addressed.

The second point has been made before but needs to be stated again. The change process cannot stop with the CEO and those who report directly to him or her. In the example above, the electronics firm's leaders are tireless in their effort to bring a rich understanding of their approach to everyone in the organization. And the 14 staff and functional heads who had spent almost two days with each other held similar meetings with their own direct reports, each of whom then held similar meetings with their direct reports, until the entire organization was reached.

Regardless of the method, the decisions that require fundamental theory change will invade the comfort zones of many managers and employees. Enduring change, therefore, will require the commitment of the senior executives. That commitment must be buttressed by their rich understanding of its implications and by their tenacious patience to see it through.

Trust—a concept as old as mankind—seems to have been newly discovered by business. In some instances, it has become a new buzzword with the attendant unfortunate consequences. In other instances, businesses are thoughtfully replacing the causes of mistrust with new theories, new structures, and new processes, which will reduce waste, eliminate needless complexity, and encourage creative, productive effort. Trust is the lubricant that helps them compete effectively in terms of cost, quality, and time. Other businesses that continue to carry the burdens of mistrust will have difficulty keeping up with those who have lighter loads, who are finding that trust not only liberates profits for today, but ensures the vitality that is required for tomorrow.

Epilogue

If everyone in your organization knew what to do; when, how, where to do it—and, most important, why he was doing it—what would the organization chart look like?

If everyone desired to do his job correctly, on time, *and* could be trusted to act with integrity in support of the firm's aims and goals—what would your organizational process and control systems be like?

If pride in work or accomplishment, rather than profit maximization, were the driving motivation of the firm, would your profits be more or less?

Bonus Burgers: An Exercise in Accountability and Control

The cases which follow represent actual situations which I have observed. Not all come from the same firm; obviously, they have been disguised. They usually evoke lively discussion in our Columbia executive seminars.

Where's the Beef?

You are national sales manager of a fast food chain. Incentive pay can potentially be up to 40 percent of compensation for your regional, divisional, and restaurant managers. Last week, Hurricane Hugo hit South Carolina, and the big earthquake hit San Francisco and Oakland. Do you adjust the incentive targets for these two divisions? What criteria do you use?

Frosted Buns

Company history shows that cold weather hurts sales in spring and summer. One degree below normal for the period hurts sales by 1 percent, two degrees by 3 percent, and three degrees by 5 percent. In April, the Boston region's temperatures were 5 percent below normal; Providence, Rhode Island's were below by 3 percent; and New York's by 1 percent. And, according to your New York division manager, unemployment in his area rose substantially in April. What adjustments do you make? What reasons do you give for your decision?

I Don't Want Any Cheese, I Just Want Out of This Trap

Your Providence division has 20 locations covered by the Providence media. A customer in one of the locations reported finding part of a mouse in his burger. The event was widely covered, and sales for the month were 20 percent off plan in the entire division. What adjustments do you make in the targets for the incentive compensation plan? What actions do you take regarding the Providence division manager? What action do you take regarding the manager of the restaurant where the partial mouse was reported?

Busted Burger Budgets

As New York regional manager, you submitted your 1991 budget late in 1990. No new locations were planned, and New York's economic situation was projected to deteriorate substantially. You did not believe you could put through any price increases, so you submitted what you thought was a stretch budget: sales and profits the same as 1989. You received a terse note from headquarters: "If you're not going forward, you're going backward. Take a fresh look and resubmit." You duly submitted a 7 percent sales and a 5 percent profit increase over 1989. Grudgingly, headquarters approved your budget. In April, McDonald's introduced chicken fajitas with saturation television advertising, then in August introduced 69¢ burgers, a price that had not been seen for years. Your headquarters had not come through with any new menu items, and, although they beefed up the advertising, they were no match for Big Mac. By October, you were not only behind the plan, but, compared to 1989, sales were off by 3 percent and profits off by 5 percent. As regional manager, what action do you take? Prepare two pieces of advice to the regional manager, two pieces of advice for the national sales manager, and two pieces of advice for headquarters.

Burgermeister

As an observer of these joyful scenes, you have noticed that the national sales manager spends 60 percent of his time making adjustments, adjudicating disputes, and listening to complaints. Please prepare three pieces of advice on how he might better use his time.

Seminar participants almost universally agree that relief should be given to the hurricane and earthquake victims. Not only are these acts of God, but also force majeure. What participants do not know is that those locations on the fringes that received little damage were swamped with business. Should their targets be adjusted upward?

There's startlingly little disagreement on the "frosted buns" case. Yes, weather is an act of God, but one we should be able to cope with. The plea from the New York region turns them off. "The economy is a fact of life."

Some perplexed looks accompany the reading of the "mouse" case. Participants are usually split 50-50 on whether adjustments should be made. However, by now, some of the participants are beginning to wise up to the devious nature of their instructor. Some have said they felt they were being "set up."

The budget case sets their teeth on edge. Most of them are middle managers in the process—givers and takers of budget angst. Because these participants have reached managerial ranks, they generally are unsympathetic to the plight of the regional manager. They expect the manager to be less passive—face facts, then do everything possible to make the numbers. By now, they are coming to the general conclusion that the instructor espouses—all the players are focusing on the wrong thing. "Burgermeister" poses the central questions. One, "Is this what managers are supposed to do?" and two, "What has gone wrong?"

Accountability when narrowly defined and numerically expressed tends to be limiting. It focuses attention inward—on intrafirm relationships. Supervisors become enemies—the game becomes "How do I win the battle—or at least cope?" Underperforming employees become the enemies of the supervisors. "I could have made my numbers if those turkeys had made theirs."

A sense of defeatism runs throughout these cases. If we were to collect the energy, effort, creativity, and just plain hard work committed to these intramural activities, then redirect all that power to serving the customer better, the "numbers" would go out of sight. Rather than watch thermometers, the location managers in the "frosted buns" case should have made sure that the store was sparkling, the employees eager, competent, and friendly, the outside premises orderly, the external signs and promotional pieces properly displayed. How about a few visits to local businesses promoting the quality of the food and the convenience of getting it? "Just call in your order, we'll have it ready for you." The mouseketeers had a different problem—but not insoluble. Certainly, they should not invite the media in to demonstrate how many mice they did not have—that would be tantamount to telling children not to put beans up their noses. But strict attention to fundamentals, some special promotions held at a decent interval after the alleged mouse's funeral, would be salutary.

Certainly these managers did not have control over force majeure, the weather, mouse sightings in other stores, or the competitive moves described in the budgeting case. But the managers should be held accountable for those energies and activities listed in the preceding paragraph. However, the focus on incentive compensation as a surrogate for good management has permitted—perhaps encouraged—the managers to focus on the bonus instead of the business. The compensation concept proposed in Chapter 5 should help refocus their attention on the customer rather than on the unproductive behavior we have observed.

Feed the Winners— Starve the Losers

You have just been appointed general manager of a troubled division of a mildly troubled parent company. Your division's contribution before corporate charges has been negative for the past two years, and you have been a cash user. You manufacture two product lines: One is a line of automotive radio antennae in three styles or configurations, which you sell to automotive manufacturers, dealers, and automotive supply stores. You also manufacture light-bar kits in 20 styles or configurations for pickup trucks, which are sold through truck dealers and supply stores. You have been able to gather the following information so far:

	Light bars	Antennae
Your average selling price per unit	$100.00	$10.00
Material cost/unit	40.00	1.00
Direct labor/unit	7.00	1.50
Units per year		
Through dealers	10,000	40,000
Through supply stores	90,000	260,000
To manufacturers	0	400,000
Total:	100,000	700,000
Average inventory	90 days	20 days

The antennae operation requires about 20 percent of the floor space, and the light-bar operation requires 60 percent. You are considering a proposal to use the remaining space for a new light-bar line, which will be dedicated exclusively for General Motors trucks. You anticipate that 80 percent of these units will be sold directly to General Motors factories for $80 per unit, and the other 20 percent to General Motors truck dealers for $100 per unit. Your sales force believes that they can sell 20,000 units the first year. Equipment installation for the new line will cost less than $300,000. The space is free. The light-bar line is basically an assembly operation. The antennae require extrusion and machining operations, as well as assembly.

Your division employs 40 salespeople, 3 of whom call on automotive manufacturers, the rest of whom call on dealers and supply stores. At present, you are selling to 3000 supply stores and 1000 dealers. Your total SG&A is 21 percent of revenues. Your manufacturing facility uses a single overhead burden rate of 4 times direct labor.

Your parent company has said it would fund the new line if you could produce adequate justification. But after a reasonable investment period, you will be required to produce positive cash flow at the rate of $100,000 per month, beginning six months from now. Additionally, in your second year, you will be required to produce $1.8 million in pretax contribution to corporate headquarters, or the plant will be closed. You have heard that turnaround managers with limited resources "feed the winners and starve the losers," but you are not comfortable with your present cost information. You will not be able to determine accurate costs quickly but have organized a five-person task force to begin the process. Your first meeting with them starts in ten minutes. You have decided to open the meeting with these questions:

What do we know?

What do we need to know?

How do we find out?

The seminar participants chew over this problem for two or three hours and come up with more questions than answers.

For instance, profit and loss accounting would place a value only on the inventory produced, not the total cost of designing, building, selling, and collecting for it. Return on investment calculations usually do not account properly for so-called soft development costs. Traditional accounting would ignore the relative complexity and cost of selling through 3000 auto supply stores. It would ignore the selling and travel costs, the cost of supervision for the salespeople, the cost of promotional literature and trade advertising, the cost of the semiannual sales meeting, the administrative costs of handling payrolls, benefits, settling the lawsuits caused by accidents on the road, et cetera. Traditional cost accounting would ignore the complexity and cost of approving and monitoring the credit history of each account, the cost of setting up an account, establishing its presence with order entry, accounts receivable, and distribution. Traditional accounting would not normally track the complexity and cost of distribution and shipping—selecting and packing small orders, planning for multiple drops, dealing with LTL (less-than-truckload) lots, or with UPS. Furthermore, the same administrative costs of setting up the account would be necessary also for the distribution center. Moreover, traditional accounting would not capture the differential in inventory turnover—light bars versus antennae.

Now, let us examine the effect that distribution strategy has on manufacturing costs. Selling to a large number of retail accounts will complicate scheduling, will usually lead to smaller production runs, and, sooner or later, will require special runs, particularly if some of the customers are large retailers whose purchasing power tends to command special attention.

The foregoing is not to suggest that the company strategy, perforce, should be to sell only to OEMs (original equipment manufacturers) or to avoid the complexity of multiple setups and smaller runs. Nor does it mean that the company should avoid the complexity-driven costs of selling, administering, and distributing to relatively small accounts. Indeed, the managers might wish to avoid the risk of selling only to OEMs. Whom they sell to is a strategic decision—but in order to make good decisions managers must know as much as possible about all their cost drivers, not just the traditional cost of goods percentage with SG&A (selling, general, and administrative) costs all lumped together.

The foregoing are sins of omission. Now, we come to an almost unforgivable sin—a sin of commission. The task that management and cost accountants are supposed to perform well—value the inventory—they often do wrong also. Instead of carefully measuring all the manufacturing costs and assigning them correctly to specific products and services, they use various allocation methods which invariably mask the true and total costs of production. In many U.S. companies, the plant burden (overhead) is spread by a single-number multiplier, usually direct labor, sometimes units produced or dollars of revenue received. (In service companies, overhead is allocated similarly—usually by a revenue indicator.) A significant number of companies studied by Robert Howell in 1985 spread their plant burden by direct labor. Here is an example of the outcome of using this method. If direct labor costs are $25 and the plant burden is four times direct labor, then the total plant cost is calculated to be $100. In theory, this total cost is divided by the number of units produced to arrive at a unit cost.

Thus, the total cost of plant overhead for our troubled company is $7 million. The allocated overhead for light bars is $2.8 million ($7 direct labor × 4 × 100,000 units), and for antennae is $4.2 million ($1.50 direct labor × 4 × 700,000 units). Of course, actual labor dollars can be captured for each product, then aggregated and divided into total overhead in order to arrive at a multiplier. The outcome is essentially the same. Regardless of the method, can you really believe this is the true overhead cost for each of these products when light bars require 60 percent of the plant space and probably an enormous amount of materials-handling support? However, the extrusion and machine operations for antennae might require higher energy costs. The issue is "Who knows?" The people on the plant floor probably have a better idea of true costs than the executive who is trying to make decisions from accounting reports.

But no one will know with reasonable certainty, unless the costs are assigned as a result of observation, rather than allocated as a result of gross estimation. Recent management accounting techniques will help managers have a better idea of product or service costs. Moreover, some of these techniques will help managers determine which customers are profitable and which are not. The best-known technique is called ABC (activity-based accounting). ABC is generally helpful with product costs, usually not as helpful in determining customer profitability. Some firms tend to overcomplicate ABC. They attempt too much precision, and they tend to capture and track the costs too often. In extreme instances, the cost has outrun the benefit. A simplified ABC process will ameliorate this problem. My own preference is resource-based accounting, a method developed by Robert Howell. This method is easier to use, helps managers get a better fix on customer as well as product profitability, but most importantly, tends to be proactive. It does not stop with measuring costs, it helps managers determine better methods of managing costs.

Appendix **C**

Conducting the Measurement and Control Audit

Unnecessary reports, measurements and controls can be removed by several methods. Crisis turnaround managers sometimes find that, with respect to internal reports, it is best to start with a clean slate. For instance, I abolish memoranda for the first 30 days of the turnaround. GAAP (generally accepted acounting practice) reporting is deemphasized in favor of cash projections. Productivity analyses and other management reports are eliminated if they are not directly related to cash collections or getting and keeping profitable customers. Even the time-honored sales call report is replaced by conference calls with all the salespeople hooked up. Other written reports are replaced by 4:30 p.m. daily debriefings with all hands present that are involved in information gathering and decision making. Those who are on the road are plugged in on the conference phone. Decisions need to be made quickly but wisely. This requires that the key players come face to face using interactive processes in an open, trusting environment where the aim, mission, vision, values, goals, and objectives are clearly understood. Paper only rarely contributes to this process.

For companies not in crisis, it is important to eliminate the nonsense but to preserve that which is useful. For that reason, I propose a measurement and control audit, which builds on the firm's strengths and will provide a foundation for improvement.

Itami[1] has written thoughtfully about the hidden assets of the firm—the systems and procedures which are useful, well-understood and followed, whether or not they are written down. The information relationship between suppliers and customers needs to be preserved, as well as many of the systems that they are comfortable with.

On balance, however, most companies can easily cut in half the number of measurements, reports, and formal and informal mechanisms. Even greater reductions can come from process and structural changes which simplify how the firm conducts its business.

Reorganization of process or structure, as well as the internal audit, to be enduring, must be conducted by managers and workers of the company—not by an outside consulting firm. Consultants can be scorekeepers and process coaches. They can do some of the analysis. But if the firm's own people are not the prime movers, the necessary understanding will not be gained to prevent the company and its processes from warping back into its prereorganization form.

Task Force Size and Leadership. The size of the task force will depend on the size and complexity of the organization. (One large retail organization assigned 30 of its most senior executives to a task force; however, its responsibilities were broader than cataloguing and analyzing measurements and controls.) Although some staff people may participate, most of the task force members should be line managers; however, at this point it would be helpful to rehire some of those accountants that we fired in Chapter 6. Their knowledge and analytical skills will be useful adjuncts to the process.

One more caveat: The customers should be the guiding light in this quest for more trustworthy measures and controls. The task force should be able always to answer affirmatively, "Does this activity help to design, build, sell, and collect for a product or service that will get and keep profitable customers?" For example, the customer is interested in quality, which includes such attributes as performance, reliability, desirability, consistency, aesthetics, ease of use, ease of installation, service, variety, and availability. Absolutely, the customer is interested in price, but customers are also interested in total low cost. Furthermore, the customer is interested in the company's ability to innovate—to stay ahead of customer needs. Measurements and controls which affirmatively contribute to these attributes should be preserved—better still, they should be improved.

It is entirely possible that the admonition "Less is more" will contribute to improvement. True, some internal measures and controls which do not directly address these customer concerns will be necessary. But if these controls do not make a positive indirect contribution—or worse, if they are divisive to customer concerns, as many are—then they should be removed or reengineered.

Data Collection. As I stated earlier, some would suggest that the task force should begin with a *tabula rasa*—define the aim, mission, goal, and objectives of the firm—throw out all existing measurements, controls, and reports, and then take a completely fresh look at measurement and control requirements. For most companies, this is both impractical and unwise. It would discard the benefits of institutional learning. Furthermore, the uncertainty would cripple the organization's ability to change. This does not mean, however, that timidity should prevail—that only incremental improvements should be made. Big chunks of cost and complexity can be excised by a motivated and moderately courageous task force.

The firm that was mentioned earlier collected its data in the following manner: The task force was broken into 10 groups of 3 who then interviewed almost everyone in the company to learn what measurements, reports, and controls they produced or were subject to. Composition of the task force subgroups varied because two of the three interviewers were required to be "outside" observers. The third interviewer typically worked in the area that was being studied. The ten groups gathered and catalogued samples or artifacts of every measurement and control—

whether used for internal purposes or for dealings with suppliers, customers, or other outside constituencies.

Some measurements and controls were easier to identify than others. They were written documents—reports, financial statements, budgets, operating reports, distribution service levels, lost time reports, overtime reports, sales per manhour, labor as a percent of sale, productivity reports, daily sales reports, and hundreds of others. Informal measures and controls were more difficult to identify, but they were discovered by observation and guided discussions.

Two questions were asked of almost every person in the enterprise:

What reports do you receive?

What reports do you produce?

To develop the informal list, the following questions were used:

What else is important to you?

With whom do you consult during the day?

What information do you need?

What information do you pass along?

When possible, the data gatherers observed both formal and informal meetings in order put the data in context.

This internal data-gathering process started at the top of the organization and continued down the hierarchy and across the functions until everyone in the managerial or supervisory level was interviewed and until at least one of the clerical and direct workers of every activity or function was also interviewed. The most revealing data comes not just from the managers who are interviewed but from those who are doing the work. Indeed, this revelation leads to one of the reasons that so few senior executives worry about excessive measurements and controls. The higher up the ladder, the fewer measurements they deal with.

Remember that hapless store manager from Chapter 6 with his 172-item checklist? Compare him to the president of the supermarket chain. I was interested in five things on a regular basis: sales increase, return on sales, return on investment, share price, and the relative performance of key departments—meats, produce, pharmacy, and private label. Like most executives, I received my key item reports without a true appreciation of the effort it took to produce them. Similarly, I lacked understanding of the preparation efforts or uses of the thousands of other reports in the enterprise.

Clearly, many of these reports were useful. But, useful to whom? How often should they be produced? Do they really need to be written, or can they be communicated orally? Do they really need to be stored in file cabinets and computer memory? These will be the questions that will emerge as the data are collected. And, onerous as the task may seem, all reports at every level and every function should be listed, then catalogued by the locations in which they are found. Notes should be made on each of the samples identifying where the report was found, who originated it, who received it, who else was affected by it, and how it was used.

Measurement and Control Drivers

The financial area will be a gold mine. Here the aggregate reports should be catalogued—but the individual reports that are rolled into the aggregate should also be tracked and recorded. (By eliminating one aggregate report, a dozen others might be eliminated.) The controller will be the mother lode, but the treasurer, the CFO, and *their* direct reports will yield both grains and nuggets. Internal audit reports and the proliferation of paperwork that they often demand will indeed be sobering. The fixed asset roster and attendant depreciation schedules will be wonderful to behold.

Payroll is another fruitful place to dig. The complexity in payroll departments is driven in part by tax issues and deductions for benefits. But these are not the sole drivers. Time cards—a surprisingly resilient anachronism—will also yield pay dirt. And, they will lead to the personnel or human resources department, where among hundreds of other measurements and controls, the full employment act for human relations personnel will be found. These will be the written job descriptions, job classifications, and pay grades, as well as the annual merit reviews, which were discussed in Chapters 3 and 5. Respect for privacy will prevent taking samples from some of these documents—especially the merit reviews—but the task force should collect the forms, along with the reports of compliance and noncompliance. Samples of documentation—only some of which are legally required for promotion, demotion, or dismissal—should be collected also.

The sales department will yield the beloved call report along with the associated compliance documents. Here the task force will also find exquisitely detailed sales and market analysis documents. To the extent that these analyses provide information for improvement, they will prove to be useful; but sadly, many of these are to provide defense for a performance which might have been deemed unsatisfactory.

Manufacturing is a critically important area in which to dig. For example, a cost analysis I recently reviewed showed direct labor to be 5.9 percent and plant burden to be 24 percent. Divisional burden, associated with manufacturing, was another 14 percent. Through patient questioning, the task force was able to determine that the people in division headquarters were driving much of the plant burden through their requests for information and demands for reports. The company found that when it made a head count reduction at the division level, it triggered a corresponding reduction in wasted plant burden.

It appeared that this firm had three businesses, only one of which was producing revenues and income: the one which was manufacturing and selling. The second business was the one producing the divisional overhead, sometimes helping but generally getting in the way. The third was the "corporate" business with similar questionable benefits but concrete costs.

The data collection in finance, distribution, purchasing, manufacturing, and sales will lead to the firm's external constituencies, the most important of which are customers and suppliers. Here the task force will find some amazing documents. For example, the traditional disdain for salespeople has promoted incredible barriers for suppliers who, in theory, should be valued partners. So, finding measurement and control waste in purchasing, although not defensible, is nevertheless not surprising. What will be surprising are the hoops we make our customers jump through for the pleasure of buying from us. Credit investigation, certainly important, can be streamlined and civilized so the customers need not feel like criminals while awaiting credit approval. On the technical front, electronic data exchange (EDI) is not just a frill, but a requirement for some customers. Customer invoicing will often create anger as well as derision. It might be welcomed as a guarantee of full employment in customers' accounts payable departments, but that might not be consistent with their senior managers' goals.

The in-house legal department or outside legal counsel will provide plenty of work for the task force, particularly if the legal department is led by a timid lawyer and more particularly if the company is led by a timid CEO who defers business decisions to the legal department. The problem here will be exacerbated if the company has been guilty of or charged with well-publicized legal transgressions. In this instance, the legal tentacles will be everywhere. This siege environment may or may not be appropriate, depending on the seriousness and pervasiveness of the transgressions. Suffice it to say that trust will be an alien notion, and the residue of mistrust will be costly. In this regard, the task force should be particularly mindful of controls that may be no longer appropriate—that were instituted as the result of previous calamities.

Management information systems (MIS) and electronic data processing (EDP) and the new concept, decision support systems (DSS), will be gatekeepers for measurements and controls; however, in many companies they are also the genesis. The task force might have mixed experiences gathering data here. In one firm which I recently worked with, MIS was extremely cooperative. In another I found fierce resistance. Over time, it became clear that the hostile MIS department had utter disdain for the other functional managers. Its actions signalled a deeply held belief that MIS should initiate policy as well as disseminate and provide tools for monitoring its compliance.

The alpha and omega of all the organizational measurements and controls are the policies and procedures manuals. These manuals will be found at corporate and division levels as well as almost every department of a large bureaucratic organization. One large manufacturing company that recently went through an organizational streamlining reduced its divisional policies and procedures manuals from 15 volumes to 50 pages. It is not clear who reads the 50 pages, but it was crystal clear that no one read the 15 volumes. One of my first acts as a turn-around manager is to throw out the policy and procedures manual and replace it with hands-on, interactive processes.

Data Analysis

First pass at analyzing the data should be made by the task force. A second analysis should be done by senior managers who might want to review it individually, but who most definitely should come together to review it as a group. A third analysis should be done by representative groups from all functions and all levels of the hierarchy.

All the measurements, controls, reports, and other artifacts that have been collected should be catalogued. Each should be identified according to its source and destination. Its purpose should be noted on each document. Is it used for information, control, or performance evaluation? If other uses are found, they should also be coded. Samples of the reports should be displayed roughly in relationship to their location on the organization chart—not just for dramatic effect, but to provide a sense of their dissemination up and down the hierarchy and across functions. Measurement and control artifacts from suppliers and customers should be displayed separately; however, they will all relate in some way to a company function.

The organization chart, although helpful in describing the location of measurements and controls, does not describe the process in which they are used. The task force, therefore, should develop flow diagrams or process maps of several of the organization's important processes—say, the order entry, credit check, shipping, or invoicing process, or the customer service process, or a piece of the manufacturing process. These maps will not only diagram the process but will show the points of decision, delivery, or hand-off. In this respect, the maps help to describe the relationship of people and functions.

During the review of measurements and controls, three sets of questions should be displayed in the war room—not as a prescription for decision making, but for general guidance. The first set of questions will be those posed at the beginning of the book:

If everyone in your organization knew what to do; when, how, where to do it—and, most important, why he was doing it—what would the organization chart look like?

If everyone desired to do his job correctly, on time, *and* could be trusted to act with integrity in support of the firm's aims and goals—what would your organizational process and control systems be like?

If pride in work or accomplishment, rather than profit maximization, were the driving motivation of your firm, would your profits be more or less?

Next, the set of questions which was asked at the beginning of the chapter on measures should be displayed:

Exactly what is being measured?

When?

By whom?

For what purpose?

By what method?

Is the time order of data preserved?

How is it to be communicated?

How will it affect the activity being measured?

Have we measured costs but neglected benefits?

Have we kept the customer in view?

And the next set:

What are those things that we absolutely must control?

At what location in the organization should they be controlled?

How should they be monitored?

These questions are not to be asked or answered serially but are to provide general guidance for groups who are involved in the evaluation process.

Management Orientation

With data gathering and initial analysis completed, the most senior manager and her or his direct reports should be invited to task force headquarters for a review of findings to date. The purpose of these meetings is not to make decisions, but to provide background information. Reactions of this senior group will range from amazement and consternation to defensiveness. Thus, the CEO, aided by the task force, should reinforce the idea that this exercise is not to assign blame. Rather, the review is to provide objective data which will help the company streamline its measurement and control systems. The CEO also should emphasize that elimination of wasteful activity and concomitant costs is only one of the objectives. Another important benefit of this exercise will be the liberation of the creative energies of those in the organizations who have been burdened by excessive measurements and controls.

Several paradigms can be used to put senior managers in the proper frame of mind for the next step in the process: Jack Welch has said that he wants GE to act like a $70 billion popcorn stand. Or people should be asked to recall how simple the business was when everyone knew everyone else, talked to each other every day, knew the customers and suppliers, wasted almost no time on administrivia but set out to conquer the world by serving the customer better than anyone else. The reality is that the company probably will not be small enough to operate that informally—that indeed, some of its strengths come from its size, that some of its measurements and controls contribute enormously to its success. But the entrepreneurial memory can be held as a screen to make certain that excessive measures and controls do not endanger the firm's ability to compete.

Next, each of the people who report to the CEO should hold meetings with their direct reports, including those who supervise others or who provide staff services. The objective of these meetings is to prepare the way for the next phase and to avoid problems when people are given a cold shower of unpleasant information.

User Group Meetings

With the informational meetings concluded, the next phase can begin. A group of documents which seem to have a natural relationship and which are found in roughly the same place in the organization should be selected for further analysis. A representative group of people from every function and at every level of the hierarchy where these measures and controls occur should do the analysis. Their deliberations will include their independent assessments of how the reports are used. Are they necessary as is? Should they be modified or eliminated? Can they be combined with another? Is the frequency of issue appropriate?

The focus at the outset should be on problems the measurements may have caused within their own departments. As the meeting progresses, they should discuss how a measurement report or control in one function affects another. They might wish to prepare their own process maps or flow diagrams to better understand hand-offs and relationships.

In the early stages of these meetings, the amount of information collected will create confusion. But as in all processes of this type, patterns will emerge after a time. Participants should be apprised that confusion is normal at this juncture. And there will be some reluctance to openly disagree with procedures which heretofore were "givens." The task force representative and/or discussion leader usually can help participants overcome initial fears. When the meeting is handled properly, everyone will be participating vigorously within a few hours.

The recommendations that come from the group's deliberations might include a list of reports that group members believe can be expunged immediately. Or, they might suggest consolidation or different timing. They might want more timely reports to provide immediate feedback about some activities. In other instances, members might agree that controls are necessary now but could be relaxed if people had more training. This meeting might evoke creative discussions about how measurements that are used for purposes of individual or group evaluation are unfair and sometimes reward nonproductive behavior. Participants might muster up their courage to suggest that enough trust already exists for certain onerous controls to be removed. They might even suggest how they can use peer pressure to reduce inappropriate behavior. They will make suggestions about moving the controls to different levels or functions in the organization.

All their suggestions should be written down and saved. This is the raw material for the grand redesign. However, the task force should not be required to wait for the grand design. Some of their recommendations can be acted on immediately, thus providing reinforcement that their efforts are important.

Task Force Recommendations

After recommendations are received from the user groups, task force meetings should be held frequently. During these meetings other patterns will emerge. Initial insights will be replaced by clearly stated hypotheses which should be reviewed with those who would be directly affected by any changes that are made.

During this phase of the work, the task force should have regular access to the senior management group in order to report on progress to date and to receive guidance or recommendations on those issues which are difficult to implement or which will require a change in present policies and procedures. By this time, it will have become clear that measurements and controls are more than artifacts. They are active ingredients of the system. It will have become equally clear that one part of the system cannot be changed without affecting other parts of the system. It follows, then, that changes in measurements and controls will call for changes in management methods, policies, and practices.

One of the conclusions that invariably emerges from this effort is that many excesses are driven by the control requirements of the chain of command and the coordination requirements among functions. More than three-fourths of the paper and informal communications probably will be dedicated to these purposes. Indeed, excessive measurements and controls, the loss of time, and the loss of efficiency of communication in the traditional structure has been one of the prime movers toward the new management methods which go around traditional organization structures—simultaneous engineering, tiger teams, cross-functional task forces, the diagonal slice that not only crosses functions but involves all levels of the hierarchy.

But shortening the chain of command, reducing the number of functions, blurring the boundaries in the hierarchy or between functions, or starting task forces or tiger teams will not produce to their true potential if people do not trust each other, their bosses, or the organization. If some members of the group are incompetent, if the measurement and reward system pits people against each other and against the firm, defensive or aggressive behavior and their artifacts—excessive measurements and controls—will continue to flourish.

Yes, the task force can recommend changes—removal of excessive measurements and controls, and improvement of communication and coordination. But constant vigilance of management will be required to keep things in place if the real causes are not addressed.

Postscript: Graphic Presentation

One problem with measurements and controls is the method in which they are communicated. Every manager has sat through a financial review in which interminable discussions were held in order to understand what is behind the numbers. "Sales are down by 3 percent this month" is not useful for problem solving. Moreover, it might not reflect a problem that can be solved in the usual manner. If, however, sales data are presented graphically by week, day, or month, whichever is appropriate for the specific business situation, and if they are presented over a relatively long period—say two or three years—patterns and trends may emerge that would give greater insight into this month's performance. Moreover, they should be presented also graphically by units as well as dollars, by territory, by customer, or any other grouping that properly reflects the business situation. Furthermore, notation should be made on the graphs which describes conditions under which sales were made. For instance, for a retailer, the legend "Snowstorm this week in the northeast" will add enormously to understanding. Or, "Three stores opened in Boston this week, chainwide circular distributed by Shoprite," etc. Graphic presentation saves time and arguments during the performance review. Second, it usually reveals that the most recent data point—the 3 percent drop in sales—is not unusual and as such should not be treated with a one-time promotional shot. Rather, if sales are to move upward consistently, then fundamental changes need to be made. Perhaps pricing strategies should be reviewed, merchandising mix improved, stores remodelled, store hours extended, etc. It is a job of management to make the system or process changes; yet too often, in attacking the most recent data point, managers shift the blame to store managers, merchandise managers, and others who certainly affect the system but who cannot change it.

Endnotes

Preface

1. Kenneth J. Arrow, *The Limits of Organization*, W. W. Norton, New York, 1974, p. 23.
2. George Stalk and Thomas M. Hout, *Competing against Time: How Time Based Competition Is Reshaping Global Markets*, Free Press, New York, 1990, pp. 58–59.
3. Michael Hammer, "Reengineering Work: Don't Automate, Obliterate," *Harvard Business Review*, pp. 104–112, July–August 1990.
4. F. Timothy Fuller, "Eliminating Complexity from Work: Improving Productivity by Enhancing Quality," *National Productivity Review*, pp. 327–344, Autumn 1985.
5. Tom Peters, *Liberation Management: Necessary Disorganization in the Nanosecond Nineties*, Knopf, New York, 1992.

Acknowledgments

1. W. Edwards Deming, *The New Economics for Industry, Government, Education*, MIT Center for Advanced Engineering Study, Cambridge, Mass., 1993.

Chapter 1

1. Harry Levinson, *The Great Jackass Fallacy*, Division of Research, Graduate School of Business Administration, Harvard University, Boston, 1973.
2. Kaoru Ishikawa, *What Is Total Quality Control? The Japanese Way*, Prentice-Hall, Englewood Cliffs, N. J., 1985, p. 31.

3. Dr. White's statement was made at the Conference of Educators, CEOs, and Professionals, hosted in Cincinnati in August 1991 by Procter & Gamble.

4. Some debaters use the artifice of making the other's case, albeit lamely, only to demolish it with their own argument, but this practice confirms the hypothesis.

Chapter 2

1. Joel Brockner, "Managing the Effects of Layoffs on Survivors," *California Management Review*, pp. 14–15, Winter 1992.

Chapter 3

1. W. Edwards Deming, *Out of the Crisis*, MIT Center for Advanced Engineering Study, Cambridge, Mass., 1982, pp. 121–124.

2. Kaoru Ishikawa, *What Is Total Quality Control? The Japanese Way*, Prentice-Hall, Englewood Cliffs, N.J., 1985, pp. 63–64.

3. Walter A. Shewhart, *Statistical Method from the Viewpoint of Quality Control*, The Graduate School, The Department of Agriculture, Washington, D.C., 1939.

Chapter 4

1. Of course, man often makes rational decisions, but he is not guided by his head alone. For a superb discussion of rationality in the economic sense, see *Why People Buy*, by John O'Shaughnessy (Oxford University Press, New York, 1983, chap. 5), and *Explaining Buyer Behavior: Central Concepts and Philosophy of Science Issues*, also by O'Shaughnessy (Oxford University Press, New York, 1992, chap. 5).

2. See Douglas McGregor, *The Human Side of Enterprise*, McGraw-Hill, New York, 1985.

3. See Peter F. Drucker, *Management: Tasks, Responsibilities, Practices*, Harper and Row, New York, 1973, 1974, chap. 19.

Chapter 5

1. Management by objectives as described by Peter Drucker in *Management: Tasks, Responsibilities, Practices* (Harper and Row, New

York, 1973, 1974, chap. 34) is a sensible tool. The corrupted version, management by the numbers, is not.

2. This concept, proposed by C. I. Lewis in *Mind and the World Order* (Scribner's, New York, 1929; reprinted by Dover Editions, 1956), was introduced to me by Dr. Deming and is one of the four cornerstones of the theory of profound knowledge.

3. Students of statistical theory will recognize that there is variation even in the precision described here. In fact, variation exists everywhere. It is our duty to recognize what kind of variation we are dealing with, then to reduce it either by removing special causes or, more often, by improving the process that produces the variation.

4. See Appendix A for a set of case situations on accountability that is used in my executive seminars at the Columbia Business School.

5. Another variable is the amount of total compensation, made up of medical benefits and retirement pay. Still another is the decision whether the bonuses should be in cash, some form of equity, or both. Equity participation has much to recommend it. However, the decision is far too complex to be discussed in this book. The intent here is not to design a specific plan but to lay out issues and alternatives.

6. Joel Brockner, "Managing the Effects of Layoffs on Survivors," *California Management Review*, pp. 9–28, Winter 1992.

Chapter 6

1. Though I am aware of the argument that low profit expectations and relatively low cost of capital worked to the Japanese's benefit, that does not, however, tell the whole story. Low operating costs also helped to foster improvements.

2. "Feed the Winners and Starve the Losers" is the title of an article written by the turnaround expert Donald Bibeault.

3. Galvin's statement was made at the Conference of Educators, CEOs, and Professionals, hosted in Cincinnati in August 1991 by Procter & Gamble.

4. Lowell L. Bryan, *Breaking Up the Bank*, Richard D. Irwin, 1988, chap. 2.

Chapter 7

1. These assertions will be developed in some detail in this chapter and will be expanded in Chapters 9 and 10 where we discuss com-

petence and hierarchical control. A method for rationalizing both measurements and controls is proposed in Appendix C.

2. As I was writing this, I was notified that a company had cancelled an executive seminar that I was teaching because travel budgets had been reduced. Department managers, wisely looking out for their own careers, did not wish to use the travel budget for continuing education. The decision to cancel executive education could have been the correct decision but not as an unintended consequence of controlling travel budgets.

3. John O. Whitney, *Taking Charge: Management Guide to Troubled Companies and Turnarounds*, Business One Irwin, Homewood, Ill., 1987, reprinted by Warner Books, 1992, p. 11.

4. Erich Fromm, *Escape from Freedom*, Holt, Rinehart, and Winston, New York, 1941, p. 134.

Chapter 8

1. Mary Anne Devanna, Associate Dean for Executive Education at Columbia Business School, introduced me to the idea of the permeable organization structure, where ideas and information flow freely across functions and up and down the chain of command.

2. Ernest Friedrich Schumacher, *Small Is Beautiful: A Study of Economics As If People Mattered*, Blond and Briggs, London, 1973.

3. See Tom Peters, *Liberation Management: Necessary Disorganization in the Nanosecond Nineties* (Knopf, New York, 1992), for case histories on big companies that are breaking into smaller units.

4. Brewster Ghiselin, ed., *The Creative Process: A Symposium*, University of California Press, Berkeley, 1985.

5. Michael Hammer, "Reengineering Work: Don't Automate, Obliterate," *Harvard Business Review*, p. 104, July–August 1990.

6. Peters, *Liberation Management*.

7. Hammer, "Reengineering Work."

8. C. K. Prahalad and Gary Hamel, "The Core Competence of the Corporation," *Harvard Business Review*, p. 79, May–June 1990.

9. George Stalk, Philip Evans, and Lawrence E. Shulman, "Competing on Capabilities: The New Rules of Corporate Strategy," *Harvard Business Review*, p. 57, March–April 1992.

Chapter 10

1. Tom Peters, in *Liberation Management: Necessary Disorganization in the Nanosecond Nineties* (Knopf, New York, 1992), makes a strong case for projects teams with professionals who come in for one assignment and leave for another. When they are truly professional and well-led, they can perform many excellent services and types of activities. My recommendations do not address the firm that is looking for excellence from a group of professionals on a specific project. The firm that uses part-timers to augment ongoing activities and that is looking only to save money will be sorely disappointed.

2. Theodore Levitt, *Thinking about Management*, Free Press, New York, 1991.

3. W. Edwards Deming, *Out of the Crisis*, MIT Center for Advanced Engineering Study, Cambridge, Mass., 1982, p. 249.

Chapter 11

1. To help sensitize people to the need for change, I recommend two superb books: Danny Miller, *The Icarus Paradox*, Harper Business, New York, 1990, and Eliot A. Cohen and John Gooch, *Military Misfortunes: The Anatomy of Failure in War*, Free Press, New York, 1990. Excerpts from these provide substantive grist for discussion.

2. Other case histories that were used in this book have been disguised, but the electronics distribution firm is so well known that its identity should be shared. The firm is Marshall Industries of El Monte, California, and the COO is Rob Rodin who, with the CEO's enthusiastic support, has implemented the changes that were described.

Appendix C

1. Hiroyuki Itami, *Mobilizing Invisible Assets*, Harvard University Press, Cambridge, Mass., 1987.

Index

About the Author

John O. Whitney is director of the W. Edwards Deming Center for Quality Management and a professor at Columbia University's Graduate School of Business, where his course on managing turnarounds is among the most popular on campus. His previous book, *Taking Charge: Management Guide to Troubled Companies and Turnarounds*, grew out of his successful work as chairman, president, or director of half a dozen turnaround companies.

SOURCES

M   Misalignment of measurements and rewards—pits people against one another and against the firm.   ⟶

I

S   Incompetence or the presumption of incompetence, whether bosses, peers, or subordinates.   ⟶

T

R   Imperfect understanding of systems, causing activity that diverts effort from the organization's goals.   ⟶

U   Information that is biased, late, useless, or wrong.   ⟶

S

T   Lack of integrity.   ⟶